Expressive DRAWING

A Schematic Approach

Nancy Foote, *Study,* **brush and pen, 10" x 15" (25.5 x 38 cm)**

Expressive DRAWING

A Schematic Approach

Joseph Mugnaini

Davis Publications, Inc.

Worcester, Massachusetts

This one is for two
Lena Gibbs and Albert Porter

Copyright 1988
Davis Publications, Inc.
Worcester, Massachusetts, U.S.A.

Printed in the United States of America

Library of Congress Catalog Card Number:

ISBN: 0-87192-207-X

Graphic Design: Penny Darras-Maxwell
Cover Drawings: Joseph Mugnaini

10 9 8 7 6 5 4 3 2 1

Contents

Foreword

WHAT MORE CAN I SAY about Joe Mugnaini, illustrator of many of my books, that I haven't already said? How about...that he moves from strength to strength impelled by his imagination—from drawing to painting to writing.

Writing. Standing back with the naked eye or moving in close with a crystal lens, Joe Mugnaini inspects the panorama of graphic expression. His judgments are a superb inspiration. Beauty is beauty. Junk is junk. I have seen both issue from the minds and out of the fingertips of warm acquaintances and good friends. I may not shout their inadequacies from the housetops, but neither do I offer false praise. In the case of Joe Mugnaini and *Expressive Drawing,* there is no problem: the writer, the book are here to help us understand and create that strange extension of ourselves we name as Art.

Enough.

Ray Bradbury
September 1, 1988

Introduction

Drawing is the probity of art.
Ingres

T HE HISTORY OF ART is a continuous tapestry extending from prehistory to the present. Woven within the fabric are images of the various periods, each distinguished by its own particular style. Some images are isolated; others overlap and combine into new, vigorous patterns; all eventually become part of the fabric.

The intrinsic structure of the tapestry symbolizes the human need for visual communication, which extends beyond museums and halls of history. Visual art is a method of communication that cannot be imprisoned within traditionally established academies, nor can it be diminished or compromised by current art vogues. The discovery of prehistoric art in widely separated regions of the world, exhibiting striking similarities in technique and style, suggests an emerging trend toward stylization even during those early periods. These early graphic recordings forecast the advent of an indispensable ingredient in art education— the book. Like the modern book, these prehistoric "illustrated caves" are repositories of information that provide insight into the *intangible* nature of visual expression.

In the field of visual art there are intangibles that can be presented only through indirect methods. In this book, as in the classroom, diagrams, demonstrations and examples are employed. The text contains such traditionally accepted aids as the simile, the anecdote and one of the oldest of teaching devices, the parable.

Terminology often is misleading unless it clarifies specific problems in the technical and theoretical material presented. For example, the word *element,* because of its utilitarian versatility, has been assigned a dual role. It refers primarily to the principal components of visual art: line, tone, color and texture. Alternatively, it refers to known factors that cannot be specifically defined, such as the *spatial elements* of design or the *structural elements* of form and so on.

In a classroom relationship the stimulating verbal thrust and parry between students and teacher generates a climate in which terminology may be clarified. Such a relationship cannot be developed in a book. To promote clarity I enlisted the cooperation of former students, many of whom are also involved in art education. They provided tapes and notes that were most helpful. In a sense, the graphic format of this book, its text and terminology have been "certified" by those whom I consider most qualified to do so—student-artists.

Giorgio Vasari, in *The Lives of the Painters, Sculptors, and Architects,* recounts an illuminating anecdote about Michelangelo. One morning as he passed a group of loafing apprentices, the artist, then in his eighties, was jokingly asked if he were on his way to church. He replied, "No," he was going to the academy to learn to draw. With one sentence he admonished the apprentices for wasting time and compared drawing to religion. Those who teach art will sense the aim of his response. Drawing is something that one never stops learning.

Those who have probed with pencil, pen and other media to lay bare the hidden elements of form and have struggled to master the skills of draftsmanship will agree with Ingres: the integrity and truth of art is rooted in drawing. Both Michelangelo and Ingres, in declaring the preeminence of drawing, were referring to draftsmanship, the analytical and descriptive version of drawing that has not only been separated from its monochromatic expressive counterpart, but also from the remainder of art, including painting and graphics. One has often heard a student say, "I can paint but I can't draw." Such a conclusion is questionable. To a great degree, the same factors apply to drawing as to painting.

The aim of this book is to demonstrate that visual art, like the spoken language, is an extension of human thought and that drawing is a graphic equivalent of the written language. The elements of visual art, having evolved through physical and emotional experience, are permanently impressed upon the mind of the viewer and the artist.

The book is divided into three parts. Part I, The Theory, considers drawing from the teacher's perspective. Part II, The Practice, is the heart of the book with classroom material directed toward the student. Part III, The Portfolio, is a collection of drawings, mainly contemporary, that employ many of the theories and principles presented in Parts I and II.

This example of descriptive drawing was completed as a class project in figure drawing. It was rendered with carbon stick, forerunner of compressed charcoal. Through selective observation, the student graphically described what normally is seen by the human eye. A thorough knowledge of anatomical structure and skillful handling of the medium fostered accuracy in rendering the detailed image.

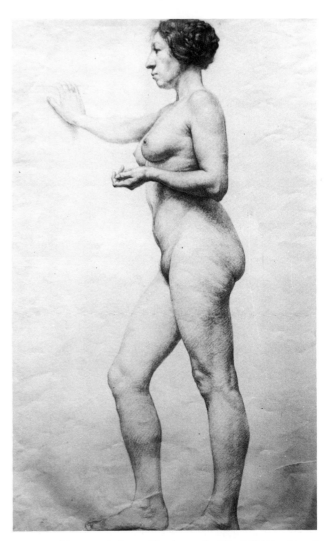

Jirayr Zorthian, *Study from Life,* charcoal, 18" x 24" (46 x 61 cm)

Rico LeBrun, *Crucifixion after Gruenwald,* **lithograph, 28" x 36"
(71 x 91.5 cm). Collection of Joseph Gatto**

In this expressive drawing Rico LeBrun combines ink and wash to convey a somber impression of a tragic event. Like a composer who restructures the work of another, the artist has freely interpreted in black and white a painting completed more than four centuries ago. This drawing could very well be titled *Tonal Variations on a Theme by Mathias Gruenwald.*

The rhythmic, convoluted patterns of the expressive drawing by Christine Taylor Patten (opposite page) were spontaneously conceived with free calligraphic movements, later skillfully rendered in pen and ink. It is a masterful combination of draftsmanship and expressive design.

Our visual sense is designed primarily for survival in a dynamic environment. Through the agency of light, we constantly gather and store information related to form, space and motion. Through visual and physical experience we steadily reinforce an inherent ability to gather and appraise instantly the nature of an object or incident and its position in space relative to ours.

Awareness of our surroundings is made possible by comparing incoming images with data that we subconsciously have been storing throughout our lives. We can notice something wrong with the mouth in a portrait and recognize a change in appearance after a long absence from a familiar person. We subconsciously gauge and record variations in familiar shapes.

A course in drawing taps this wealth of subconscious information regarding form and space and adopts it as a base for effective draftsmanship and aesthetic expression.

Drawing is much more than a discipline to be endured in pursuit of a career in art, or a monochromatic preparation for a work to be realized in color in another medium. Whether descriptive, analytical or expressive, it is an intriguing, mind-challenging endeavor. As a visual method of communication, unlike verbal and written language, drawing is universally comprehended. Expressive drawing, which has long been subordinated to painting and graphics, is now recognized as a legitimate medium.

Christine Taylor Patten, untitled, pen and ink, 50" x 72" (127 x 183 cm)

Andrew Wyeth, *Beckie King*, pencil, 28½" x 34" (72 x 86.5 cm).
Dallas Museum of Fine Arts, gift of Everett L. De Golyer

Beckie King is a descriptive drawing with elements of expressive drawing. The general shape and detail of the image have not been copied, but have been sensitively and purposefully reorganized. Artists, like musical conductors, mute or amplify the elements with which they work. In this case, random patterns of folded drapery have been translated into gentle flowing movements that complement and emphasize the detailed texture in the exposed arm and head. The subject of this drawing is the likeness of a person, but its expressive content is an image of peace and dignity.

Drawings exist as a form of expression in their own right. The boundaries that traditionally have separated them from the rest of visual art have progressively overlapped, merged and are now practically nonexistent. A prominent example is Picasso's *Guernica,* a hard-edged "painting" done in black and white. Other examples are the mixed-media works of Egon Schiele in which ink, oil, chalk, and other media are combined on various surfaces.

The freedom either to eliminate or to add color to a work of visual art, and to mix dry, wet, opaque and transparent material should not be interpreted as an endorsement of conceptual or technical anarchy. Neither should it suggest that all the principles and methods traditionally incorporated into art education are obsolete. *Developing a graphic vocabulary still depends on the artist's ability to analyze and interpret the hidden elements of form and to master the grammar of visual art.*

Verbal and visual communication are fundamentally utilitarian; however, we have learned to employ each for aesthetic and expressive purposes. The utilitarian written language may range from a grocery list to a pamphlet on the maintenance of a vacuum cleaner. In its expressive role, the written word attains the heights of literature as in *The Songs of Solomon* and Melville's *Moby Dick.* The utilitarian

visual language may encompass a child's hopscotch game sketched in sand and the symbols of traffic signs. At the expressive extreme, visual language produces the majestic tonal passages of Rembrandt's self-portraits, the lyrical celebration of life seen in Botticelli's *Primavera* and the sophisticated illustrations by Aubrey Beardsley for Oscar Wilde's plays and the strong yet sensitive work of Georgia O'Keefe.

Most follies as well as triumphs of civilization have been conceived or influenced by drawing. Drawing has been, and still is, the principal catalyst for transforming abstract concepts into concrete reality. It is difficult to imagine a cathedral being constructed from written instructions, yet the structural and aesthetic designs of architecture are realized and comprehended through drawing with the most utilitarian of the graphic elements—*line.*

Regardless of content, the potential of drawing depends upon the command of its grammar (draftsmanship), a sense of spatial organization (composition) and a concept or purpose to justify its content (design). Eventually the student-artist will realize that nature's version of reality may be bypassed and that visual phenomena can be studied for clues, revealing the invisible factors that govern the function and shapes of this world. Drawing begins in the mind.

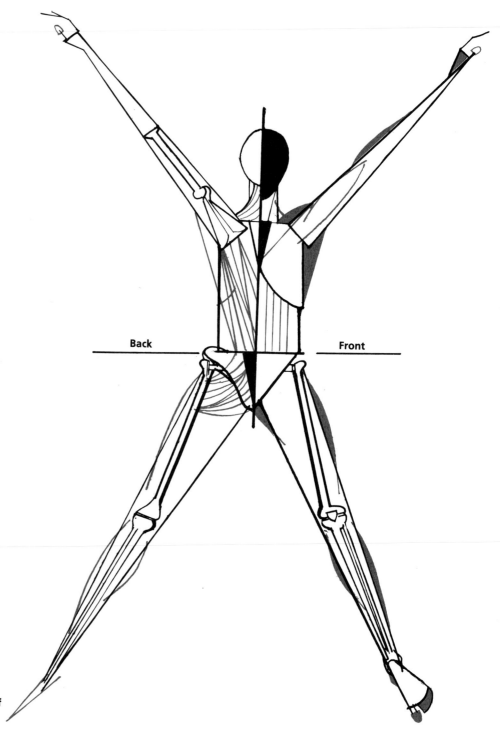

Back   Front

**Study for Schematic Structure of
the Human Figure**

Part 1

The Theory

THE FIRST SECTION of this book is concerned with the development of perceptive vision and sound draftsmanship. It shows that purposeful, consistent design finds its counterpart in the functions and forms of nature, and that visual art requires a measure of science as well as technical skill. As an example, perspective and foreshortening are based on the optical sciences, while the expressive and aesthetic potential of the visual elements (line, tone, color, texture, etc.) are rooted in visual psychology. It also directs attention to the picture plane, emphasizing the ways in which shape, proportion, and size affect the image depicted. The theories, recommended exercises, diagrams and illustrations are designed to stimulate *selective vision,* a method of viewing and conceiving form, space, and motion that lends substance to visual art regardless of its subject.

This analytical drawing is especially designed for this book. It plots the schematic design of the human limbs, the spinal column and the thoracic and pelvic girdles. Line, the principal descriptive element of visual art, describes variations in mass resulting from the inseparable relationship between function and shape. The result is similar to an engineer's blueprint.

Chapter 1

Function,

Form

and Structure

Who has seen the wind?
Neither you nor I;
But when the trees bow down their heads
The wind is passing by.
Christina Rossetti

L EARNING TO DRAW is learning to see. The beginning stages of a course in drawing are a period of discovery, a time when the student-artist finds out that draftsmanship involves more than acquiring manipulative skill and learning to imitate objects in space. She or he begins to realize that draftsmanship (analytical and descriptive drawing) and expressive drawing must penetrate the superficial appearance of visual phenomena. Artists must seek out the hidden elements of form as does a composer the elements of music. This may be accomplished only by questioning the most seductive and persuasive of the senses—sight.

Neither scholar nor artist has a covenant with the muses granting a privileged understanding or appreciation of visual art. The potential for this understanding is universally available. The Rosetta stone by which the graphic language of visual art may be interpreted is indelibly impressed within the human mind. The first impression takes place at birth when we sense the strangeness of space and scream and gesture with outrage and terror, struggling to return to prenatal security. Ironically our first "glimpse" of the world is conveyed through the sense of touch. Later, with the awakening sense of sight, we learn to associate what we see with what we have experienced through physical contact. Even at remote distances our eyes instantly translate the darks, lights and linear patterns of objects into the planes, textures and edges of forms that have become familiar through the sense of touch.

The symmetrical form illustrated here displays the close relationship between our visual and tactile senses, how both convey identical information. It is a prototype of a general symmetrical form that could be composed of semirigid material like wet clay. It is a graphic example of how the elements of line and tone are coordinated to describe form in representational art, and to emphasize the way all form must adjust to the uncompromising force of gravity. The contoured line surrounding the varying degrees of tone is a linear interpretation of expanding and receding mass from a real or imaginary core. Notice that both line and tone meet at designated points, some positive, some negative. These points mark the limits of expansion or contraction of mass, away from or toward the central core. A gradual transition of tone is matched with a continuous flowing line; a sudden reversal of either expansion or retraction is sharply delineated with angular line and *hard-edged* tone. The critical points mark the limits of the object's stability. To add mass to its positive critical point, or subtract it from its negative critical point would weaken its structure and eventually cause it to surrender to the force of gravity, to collapse. A larger version of this proto-type would require a rigid supporting armature at its center with lateral extensions to support its expanding mass. This fundamental assumption conforms to the principles adapted for the endoskeletal supporting structure of all vertebrates.

The ribbonlike structure represents a strip of paper shaped to the contour of the prototype. It demonstrates how line and tone are combined to project a graphic version of three-dimensional reality upon a two-dimensional surface.

In the diagram of a section and outline of the prototype form, part A represents a slot cut out of a piece of card-board through which we see the graduations of tone of our prototype, apart from the contoured lines. This section demonstrates that tone reveals the variations in form that confront the viewer. In contrast, B is a linear version of the limits of the object as it encounters space.

EXERCISE

Move your hand or fingers over the illustrated slot in A to "feel" as well as see the difference between the gently rounded contour, the sharply defined planes and the tex-tured base of the prototype. To complete the experiment, place a prominently defined object under a strong light angled over it at about 45°. With eyes closed, knowing the direction of the light source, feel the contours and planes of the object. You will be able to translate mentally what you feel into passages of tonality that visually describe the plastic reality of the form.

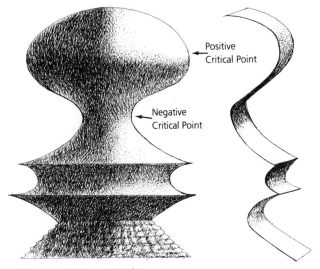

Positive Critical Point

Negative Critical Point

Prototype of Symmetrical Form

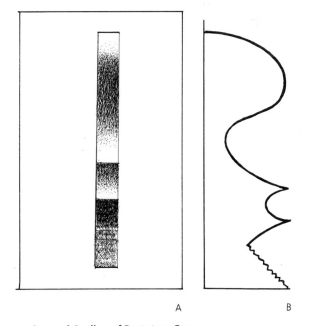

A   B

Section and Outline of Prototype Form

In the standing figure David Schnabel has coordinated a dark tone and a middle tone with a contoured line, adopting the principles shown in the symmetrical prototype. In the seated figure Corinne Hartley has "blocked out" the main planes of a female figure, following the principles shown in the section and outline diagrams.

Corinne Hartley, *Female Figure*, pen and ink, 10" x 10" (25.5 x 25.5 cm)

David Schnabel, *Female Torso*, chalk, 23" x 36" (58.5 x 91.5 cm)

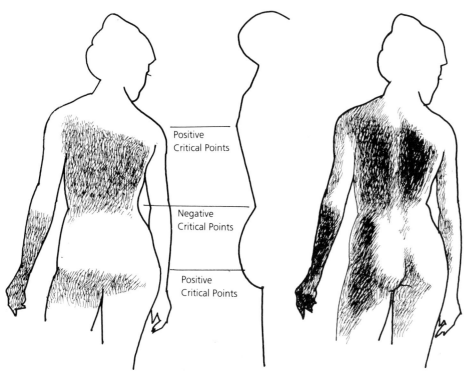

Relating Form to Tone and Line

Renzo Fenci, *Girl with Doves*, bronze, 7' (2 m)

The figures in this illustration show the relationship of form to tone and line. In the torso on the left, the principal planes that result from variations in its mass are strongly defined with tone. The contour in the center represents the principal planes defined with line. The secondary variations in the pelvic and thoracic girdles and back are indicated by introducing a deeper tone in the torso on the right.

The inseparable relationship between the tactile and visual senses is unmistakably evident when viewing sculpture. Even a brief glance at the photograph of *Girl with Doves* conveys an incredible amount of information based upon past experiences realized through the sense of touch. The viewer immediately knows its texture because surfaces of a similar nature have been felt as well as seen. The strongly defined tonal patterns that indicate expanding and receding mass could be easily identified with eyes closed. Plastic art, like visual art, is critically dependent on human visual and physical experiences with nature.

Maynard Dixon, *Tree,* **pen and ink, 12" x 12½" (30.5 x 32 cm)**

Form and Space

"As you go through life, brother, no matter what your goal, keep your eye upon the doughnut and not upon the hole" (Anon.).

In visual art, as in nature, however, the hole is as important as the doughnut. Space and its relationship to form are inseparable whether you are working to improve draftsmanship or are considering the spatial elements of composition. The following text presents concepts to help you develop a familiarity with form and space.

Nature, not the critic, sets the standards for aesthetic qualities in art. The viewer, conditioned throughout life by the efficient spatial organization observed in nature and in many man-made objects, expects harmonious composition in art. To sense and understand the relationships between space and form through draftsmanship, the normal way of viewing the subject must be reversed. Space, which is usually taken for granted, must be considered an essential element of form, whereas the attention-monopolizing outline or edges of the subject must be temporarily ignored until they are properly related to structure.

In general, form defines and occupies space in two ways. It either contains it or activates it. An example of *contained* space is the human body cavity in which the pelvic and thoracic girdles and the ribs, supported by the spinal column, surround and contain the volume necessary to accommodate the internal organs. Space is *activated* by the

Schematic Plant Forms

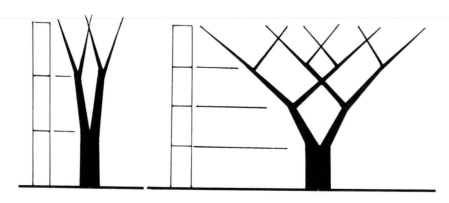

edges of adjacent forms, between closely assembled objects, hollows, projections. The space beneath an uplifted arm is activated space that could be occupied at any moment, as is the space between the stationary blades of an electric fan. The spaces between the branches, limbs and leaves of a tree are activated within an efficiently proportioned pattern designed for survival. The schematic plant forms demonstrate how space is incorporated within plant structure.

Two different plant forms are represented here. Each has its total mass divided into equal parts as it progresses through each stage of growth. The variations in the spatial pattern within each stage are dependent upon the ratio of the plant's spreading mass to the space it occupies. Starting with the compressed cylindrical shape of the trunk, an equal amount of material in each phase is progressively distributed to occupy additional space. The branches and limbs multiply in number as they gradually diminish in size, ending in a final spray of twigs and leaves. The result is a pattern of efficient spatial distribution adjusted to the uncompromising force of gravity. The formula for plant life is to mix the required proportions of leaves, moisture, sunlight and space. To accomplish this, each plant type has developed its own pace or cadence. Many, like the palm tree, extend themselves with a single thrust before ending in a final spread. Others, like the sycamore and birch, accomplish the move in three, four or more phases. In contrast, the oak requires as many as eight or ten phases. Regardless of its spatial pattern however, a tree, like most living structures, could not exist without an invisible factor that is too often taken for granted—space. The spaces between the branches, limbs, twigs and leaves of a tree are essential to its structure, its function and its life.

A growing tree is an "event." The varied movements of its branches are more than random outcroppings. The growth pattern of a tree is an artifact of efficient spatial organization. A stop-action film of the life of a tree would show a continuous dance-like adjustment to the force of gravity. A tree is the recognizable subject of Maynard Dixon's drawings, but its true content is a graphic rhythmic recording of the development of a living structure.

James Carlson, *Source*, etching, 11" x 8" (28 x 20.5 cm)

James Carlson's *Source* is an etching of a root system that gathers and distributes material essential to the life of a tree. Both branch and root systems exhibit similar patterns because of similar spatial requirements. By turning the book upside down, the branch system and root system roles will seem reversed.

Space and the Picture Plane

Visual art is the art of spatial organization. As music evolves in a measured sequence of time, so visual art manifests itself within a limited area of space—the *picture plane.* The success of any graphic project is critically dependent on the shape, size, proportion and texture of the surface upon which it is developed. With the exception of works that have been preserved as historical artifacts, the art that has endured is endowed with elements that elude definition yet display expressive qualities achieved only through skilled draftsmanship and either a trained or intuitive sense of spatial organization. This art includes the work of twentieth century innovators such as Paul Klee, Piet Mondrian and Arshile Gorky, as well as the work of the old masters— all excellent draftsmen with insight into the principles of spatial organization and design.

The accompanying illustrations demonstrate the interdependence of the subject and the picture plane. The most neutral of angular shapes, the square, has been chosen for the drawing surface. The most neutral shape known, the sphere, has been selected to represent the subject.

a. The picture plane is a flat neutral square.

b. The circle seems to emphasize the two-dimensional surface of the square.

c. The addition of a semicircle introduces the illusion of opacity. The circles now appear disc-like and three-dimensional; the square is no longer flat; shallow space is suggested. This setup exemplifies how subject matter and environment in graphic art are interdependent. *The appearance of the area of the picture plane that was untouched has been transformed by modifying the subject upon its surface.*

d. Detail changes the disc-like shapes into spheres; the space within the picture plane is deepened. Detail also *indicates the hidden opposite side of the spheres.*

e. The space illusion of between the spheres is increased by reducing the size of the sphere in the upper region of the picture plane.

Diagram of the Picture Plane

f. Infinite space is indicated by sectioning some of the spheres as they encounter the boundary of the picture plane.

g & h. Detail rotates each sphere and places it in relation to the position of the viewer.

i. Groupings of indefinite dimensions are suggested by increasing and compressing the spheres within the proximity of the limits of the picture plane. This suggests a section of densely occupied space (See *Salzburg,* by Suzanne Bravender, in Chapter 2.) The sectioned circles without detail acquire the semblance of the detailed spheres by being surrounded by them. The influence of environment upon the subject cannot be ignored.

Draftsmanship involves more than skillfully rendering a two-dimensional version of reality. It also calls for the ability to activate and control the infinite potentials for expression possible within the boundaries of the picture plane.

Two of the most commonly used visual devices are *perspective* and *foreshortening*. The diagram on perspective shows how both are combined to convey the illusion of volume and space.

A. Lines thrusting upward from the intersections suggest structures rising from the flatness of the picture plane.

B. Lines thrusting downward indicate hollowness or depth.

Gerald Brommer has adopted the visual device shown in A in his *Cathedral of Notre Dame.*

Gerald Brommer, *Cathedral of Notre Dame,* pen and ink, 12" x 18" (30.5 x 46 cm)

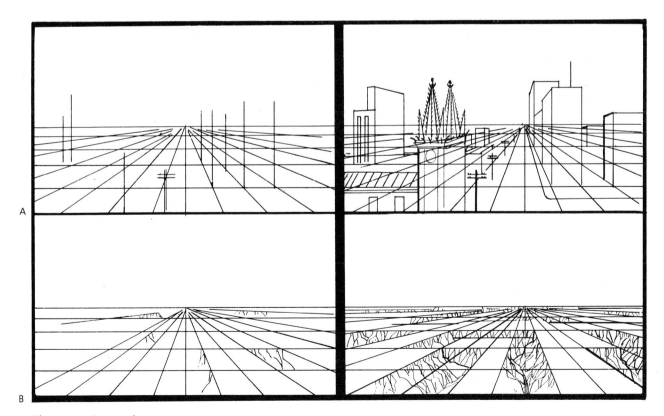

Diagram on Perspective

Chapter 2

The Elements

of Art

Little drops of water
Little grains of sand
Make the mighty oceans
and the pleasant land.
Julia Fletcher Carney

T HE PRINCIPLES of aesthetics and expressive design are based upon the physical nature and limited space of the picture plane and the manner in which it is activated by any or all of the principal *elements* of visual art. *Line, tone, color* and *texture* traditionally have been classified as the primary elements; some people include space and form in the list. However, space as an element requires special consideration. Establishing form as an element remains questionable since it is through the primary elements that it is realized.

All works of art include at least a trace of line, tone and texture, even though these elements may have been introduced inadvertently. For example, the paintings of Georges Seurat, composed of closely juxtaposed dots of pigment designed to intensify the quality of color, incorporate all of the elements, including line, which evidently he tried to avoid. William Turner, another artist whose work is not distinguished by line, included it indirectly in the softly contoured silhouettes of his subjects. On the other hand, Sandro Botticelli's work, definitely curvilinear in design, displays a moderate range of tonality along with lyrical passages of color. The paintings and etchings of Rembrandt rely mainly upon tone with the element of line assuming a supporting role. In his paintings tonal passages were developed by applying transparent glazes of black combined with a limited range of color over a white textured area. Even though the images are dominated by tone, their design is enhanced by employing, in varying degrees, the elements of line, color and texture. The dynamic imagery of Vincent van Gogh owes as much to the vigorously stroked texture of oil pigment as it does to color.

Normally student-artists gravitate toward the element that conforms to their particular requirements, eventually casting the remaining elements in either supporting or minor roles. Examples and diagrams follow that demonstrate the uniqueness of each visual element, beginning with line.

Line

The most essential element is *line*. It is a graphic symbol of spatial concepts that are not exclusive to art. The persuasive powers and descriptive potentials of line originate in nature. The spider, sensing the direction of the breeze that carries it with its extruding fibers to a predesignated location, and the bee, charting the course between its objective and the hive, are instinctively aware of the shortest distance between two points. In the remote past, the first graphic images were impressed with finger, stick and stone into the soft textured surface of earth, mud and sand. The words on this page are linear symbols of the sounds that make up the English language. With line, man has predicted and even described events and dimensions beyond the range of vision. If we were compelled to select only one of the elements to work with during the remainder of our lives, the logical choice would be line.

In the pen and ink facsimile drawing the interior and exterior proportions, volume and basic structure of a building have been indicated with line.

Rembrandt's pen and brush study demonstrates that the imagery and spatial organization (composition) of a painting is conceived with line, even though tone is to be the dominant element.

Rembrandt, *Study of Saskia Lying in Bed,* pen and brush in bistre, wash, 5³/₄" x 7" (14.5 x 18 cm). National Gallery of Art, Washington, Ailsa Mellon Bruce Fund

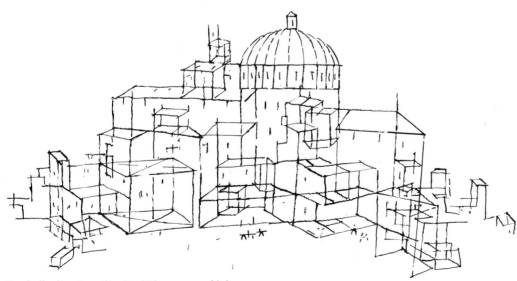

Facsimile drawing after Paul Klee, pen and ink

Outline Copy of Rembrandt, *Self Portrait*

As a class project students were asked to evaluate the influence of line in the design of several well-known paintings. Transparent tracing paper was placed over a reproduction of a painting and the students carefully traced the visible pattern of its elements with line. Three of the results are shown in the tracings of *Self-Portrait* by Rembrandt, *Venus Rising from the Sea* by Sandro Botticelli and *Self-Portrait* by Vincent van Gogh. It is obvious that line is not the principal element in the imagery of Rembrandt, nor is tone the dominant element in the lyrical design of Botticelli. It may be surprising, however, to see that the element of color in van Gogh's painting is intensified by a balanced combination of line and texture.

Line as a versatile element is unequalled. In the Rembrandt self-portrait the features of the head have been explicitly detailed with a minimum of varied linear accents later in this chapter. In Botticelli's painting the sinuous contours of the figure, rhythmic flow of hair and detail of the limbs are manifested with line. In the van Gogh self-portrait the essential components of its design are easily translated with a detached, staccato version of line.

Outline Copy of Botticelli, *Venus Rising from the Sea*

Line Copy of van Gogh, *Self Portrait*

Jeanne Heilman, *The Market Place,* **first stage of etching**

Line can be utilitarian. In the first stage of Jeanne Heilman's etching, line has been etched into the surface of a metal plate. This is the first step in developing an intaglio designed to include the remaining elements, color, texture and tone, as shown in her finished etching.

Jeanne Heilman, *The Market Place,* **finished etching, 18" x 24"**
(46 x 61 cm)

Suzanne Bravender, *Salzburg,* **pen and ink**

In *Salzburg* Suzanne Bravender has used brisk calligraphic
line to suggest an assembly of indefinite dimensions
extending beyond the boundaries of the picture plane.

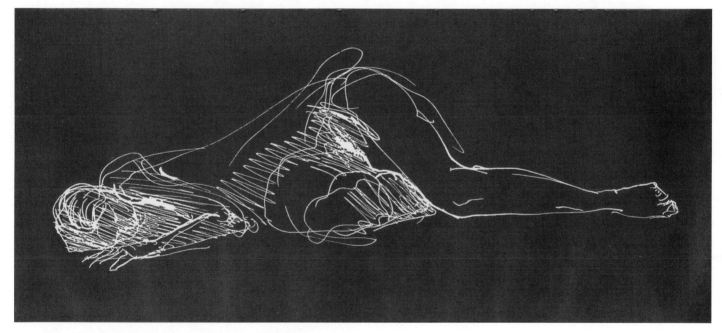

David Starrett, *Female Nude*, etching 4³/₄″ x 10¹/₂″ (12 x 26.5 cm)

In *Female Nude* a black pen and ink line has been changed to white by having it photoetched onto a metal plate, rolling printers ink on its surface and running it through a press. The medium is generally known as an etching; however, the image is realized through drawing. In this particular approach an intense white *line* is developed without being restricted by the difficulty of producing it with white pigment on a dark surface. In addition, freedom afforded by free-flowing ink is preserved.

Rembrandt, *The Mill,* oil painting, 34¹/₂" x 41¹/₂" (87.5 x 105.5 cm). National Gallery of Art, Washington, Widener Collection

Tone

The element of *tone* is versatile, adaptable and graphically explicit. Combined with line it becomes an important factor in describing or representing the physical reality of form upon a two-dimensional surface. Tone also contributes a quality to visual art that suggests mystery and stimulates emotion. Frequently the terms *tone* and *value* have been considered interchangeable or synonymous. The general tendency, however, is to regard *value* as the graduations of *tone* used in visual art, from white to black or from light to dark.

An insight into the versatility of tone can be gained by subdividing the tonal range into separate categories: the *light-to-dark* scale as exemplified by the work of Rembrandt, Goya and Albert Pinkham Ryder, and the *white-and-black scale* featured in the art of Aubrey Beardsley, Piet Mondrian and Franz Kline. (See diagrams, opposite and p. 32.)

The Mill by Rembrandt has been referred to by scholars and critics as the epitome of *chairoscuro* painting (light and dark). The absolute black of the type on this page in contrast with the pure white of the paper is a practical example of the full range of *solid* (white-and-black) *tone scale.*

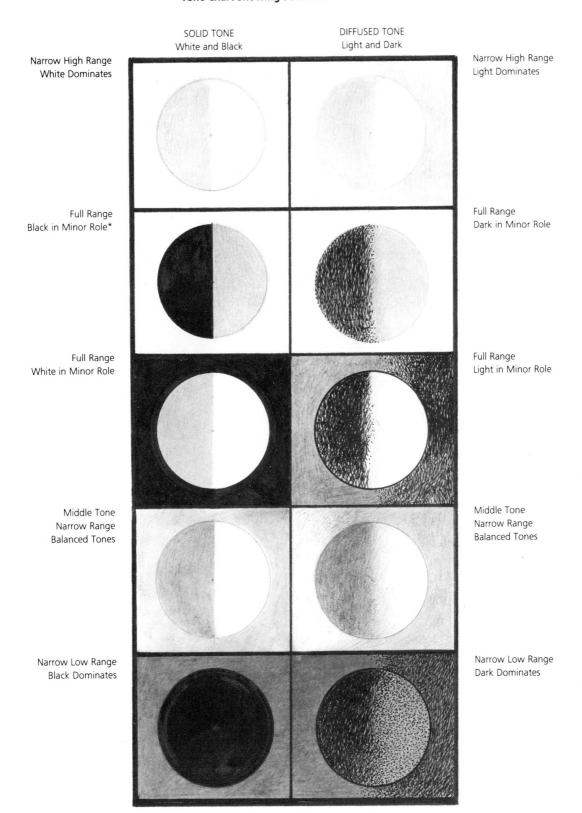

SOLID TONE
White and Black

DIFFUSED TONE
Light and Dark

Narrow High Range
White Dominates

Narrow High Range
Light Dominates

Full Range
Black in Minor Role*

Full Range
Dark in Minor Role

Full Range
White in Minor Role

Full Range
Light in Minor Role

Middle Tone
Narrow Range
Balanced Tones

Middle Tone
Narrow Range
Balanced Tones

Narrow Low Range
Black Dominates

Narrow Low Range
Dark Dominates

* A *minor role* refers to the amount of space that a value occupies, not its potential for attracting attention. Actually, the visual impression of a value is intensified by compressing it on the picture plane.

Kathe Kollwitz, *Self-Portrait Facing Right,* lithograph, National Gallery of Art, Washington, Rosenwald Collection

The tonal structure of the lithograph by Kathe Kollwitz is based on the light and dark chiaroscuro scheme. Tandra Jorgensen (see opposite page) has exploited the texture of top-graded illustration board to produce gradual transitions of tonal values ranging from the bottom to the top of the light-and-dark scale.

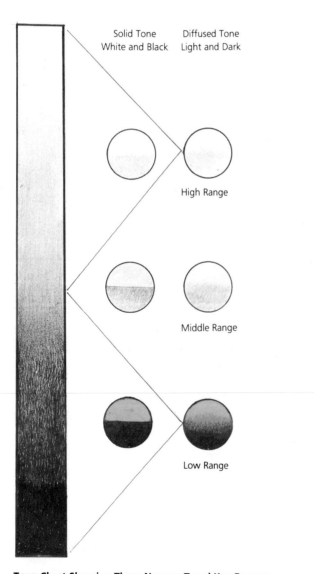

Solid Tone
White and Black

Diffused Tone
Light and Dark

High Range

Middle Range

Low Range

Tone Chart Showing Three Narrow Tonal Key Ranges

In the diagram (opposite, above) demonstrating tone on the picture plane, notice how a dot on the surface of the picture plane energizes the total area. A state has been established between the subject (the dot) and the environment (the picture plane); the area is no longer neutral. Enlarging the dot or applying more dots would not only reduce the white area, but make it, by contrast, whiter. This is an example of how opposing elements not only affect each other but support one another by emphasizing their differences. (An analogy could be the conflict between the hero and the villain in a play. By opposing each other they not only support the plot but also emphasize their differences.) The solid intense black brushstroke in the second picture plane establishes its environment, the surrounding area, as opaque white. The picture plane remains flat. In the last picture plane the fused edges of the brushstroke merging with the light value of the surface suggests transparency, atmosphere and depth. The picture plane has been deepened. The impression is a pattern of lights and darks as exemplified by the chiaroscuro imagery of Rembrandt, Goya and Caravaggio.

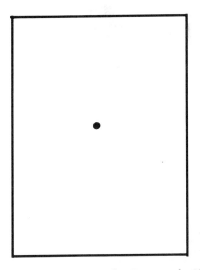  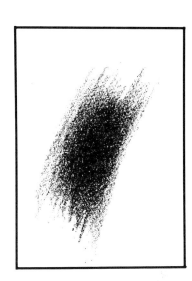

Diagram Demonstrating Tone on the Picture Plane

Tandra Jorgensen, *Skull,* **charcoal, 19¹/₂" x 25¹/₂" (49.5 x 65 cm)**

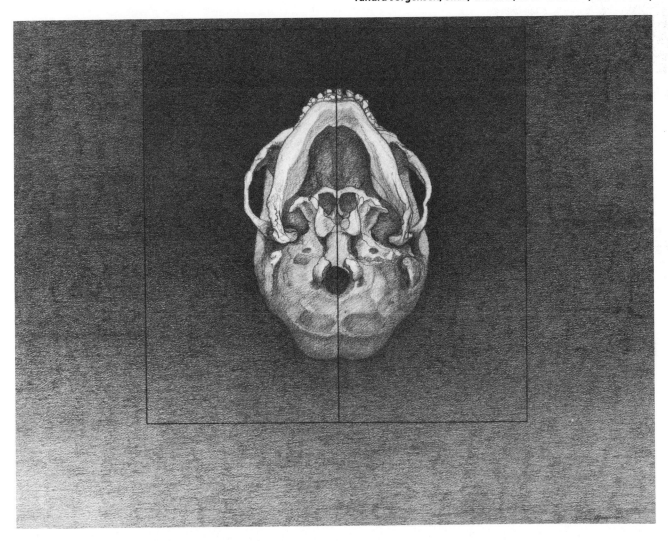

Sheila Belkin, *Bones,* **acrylic, ink and wash, 24" x 30" (61 x 76 cm)**

Nathaniel Bustion, *Eyes of the Underworld,* **intaglio, 18" x 30" (46 x 76 cm)**

The sharp-edged intaglio pattern by Nathaniel Bustion is designed in black and white. The area surrounding the figures remains in its original state, a flat white area. However, the white detail within the large pattern becomes *compressed* or intensified within the clustered environment.

In Sheila Belkin's *Bones* the full range of the solid black-and-white version of the tonal scale has been used in a pattern in which the blacks and whites are equally distributed.

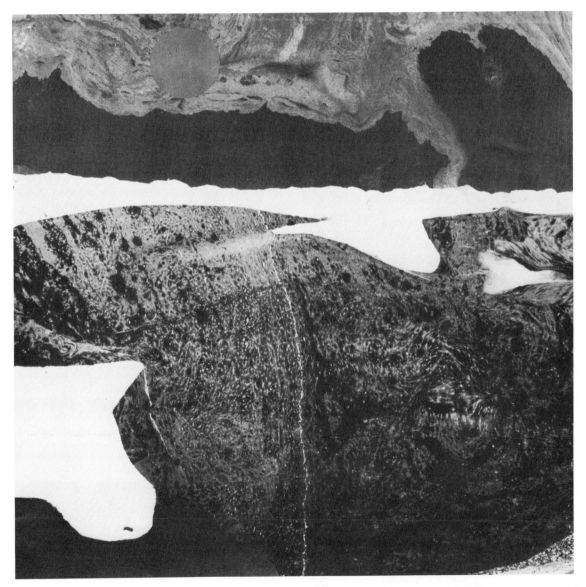

Gail Lindstrom, *Night Forms,* ink and collage, 21" x 22" (53.5 x 56 cm)

In *Night Forms,* Gail Lindstrom has contained the white areas by squeezing them from the outside. The full range of black and white has been employed.

Rembrandt, *Self-Portrait,* oil on canvas, 33¼" x 26" (84.5 x 66 cm), National Gallery of Art, Washington, Andrew W. Mellon Collection

An important breakthrough in visual art, comparable to the discovery of perspective, was the technical development of *chiaroscuro,* an Italian term for light and dark. The advent of oil pigments that could be easily manipulated allowed the artist to establish and control the volume, shape and spatial environment of a subject with what is still known as *continuous tone.* The choice of values was limited only by the extremes of the tonal scale: absolute dark, or black, and intense light, or white. However, the principles that govern consistency in design demanded then as now that the tonal composition of a work of art be contained within a *key,* a definite range of values. In *Self-Portrait* Rembrandt adopted a key consisting of the full range of the light-and-dark version of the tonal scale.

The diagram of advancing form, receding form and counterform demonstrates how a work of this type is developed through several stages. First the subject is perceived as a sphere in space, exposed to a single light source. Then the lighted area is viewed as advancing form, the darker as receding form, and the surrounding middle tone, representing space, as counterform. In the first frame a middle tone is introduced to shape the illuminated half of the sphere (*advancing form*). In the second frame a deeper value is applied to identify the half not exposed to light (*receding form*). In the third frame the tonal quality of both halves of the sphere is intensified by deepening the value of the surrounding space (*counterform*) as it encounters the lighted area, and either leaving it in its original state or

Advancing Form, Receding Form and Counterform

making it lighter as it joins the darker areas. In the final frame the basic spherical concept is ready to be modified for a specific subject, in this case, the human head.

Both *Dark Section* and *Joshua Tree Monument #8* are etchings that use the full range of the black-and-white scale. The former is abstract, the latter is semi-abstract, yet both have much in common. In both etchings black is shown in its most intense state as *color,* in the sense that color is attributed to intangible qualities present in poetry or music. The black that surrounds the isolated white areas in each work intensifies their whiteness. Work composed in the black-and-white range of the tonal scale can often be *energized* with slight variations in value without diminishing the extreme of its tonal pattern. Texture in the black as well as the white sections of the composition is activated by the subtle variations in tone that enhance the sensation of whiteness and blackness. Originally the element of line was used only to indicate the overall black-and-white pattern in these etchings, yet it is present in the sharply defined boundaries that separate the black areas from the white.

Eva and Paul Kolosvary, *Joshua Tree Monument #8,* **etching, 36" x 24" (91.5 x 61 cm)**

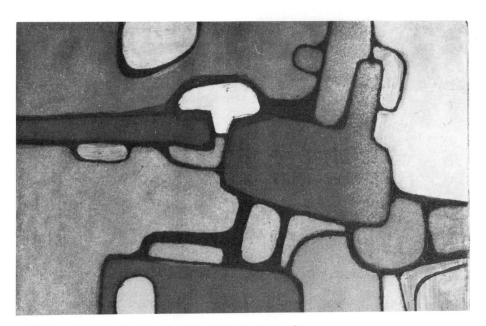

Marie Starr, *Dark Section,* **intaglio, 8" x 5" (20.5 x 12.5 cm)**

The full range of the solid white-and-black version of the tonal scale is represented by the untitled drawing by Francoise Gilot. Its design is diametrically opposed to the dark-and-light version of the tonal scale. In Rembrandt's *Self-Portrait,* for example, the viewer is firmly, yet gently directed to the focal point of the design. In contrast, the visual impact of Gilot's drawing is sudden and direct. The viewer instantly is made aware of the flat two-dimensional image. The artist has exploited the most persuasive visual device exemplified in the modern poster, in the sharp-edged, solid values of white and black at the extremes of the tonal scale. Piet Mondrian, Joseph Albers and Pablo Picasso frequently adopted a solid full-range tonal scale.

Sally Fifer Bernstein, *Trellis,* **pastel, 18" x 24" (46 x 61 cm)**

The values of *Trellis* are in the middle narrow range of the light-and-dark scale. This work is an example of well-controlled tonal design. The values within the detailed central looping pattern have been restricted to a tonal range consistent with the design, that is, the darkest value located in the upper left area of the picture plane and the lightest areas in the loop located in the middle of the right side of the picture plane.

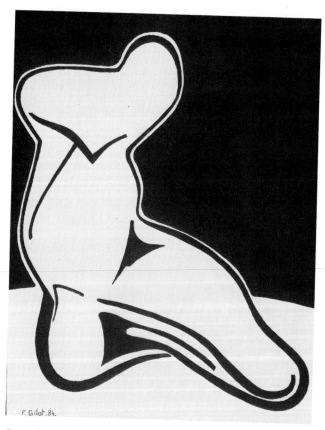

Francoise Gilot, untitled, brush and ink, 18" x 24" (46 x 61 cm)

Arshile Gorky, *The Plow and the Song,* mixed media, National Gallery of Art, Washington, Avalon Fund

The values in *The Plow and the Song* are limited to the upper narrow range of the light-and-dark scale. The darkest value, including the cursive linear pattern, is slightly above the middle tone; the lightest is close to the top of the scale.

Woman on Chair is a vignetted design in which the subject is isolated within a picture plane that is practically untouched. The figure was completed with mixed media ranging from a middle tone to scattered values at the highest level of the diffused light-and-dark scale.

The tonal values of *Figure* extend from the lowest darks to the highest lights of the light-and-dark scale. The tonal patterns in this drawing were designed to display the unique velvety blackness of compressed charcoal.

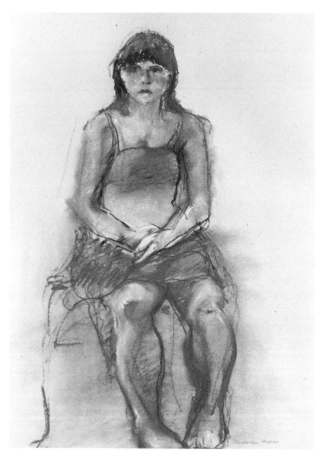

Michaele Keys, *Woman on Chair*, pastel, 18" x 24" (46 x 61 cm)

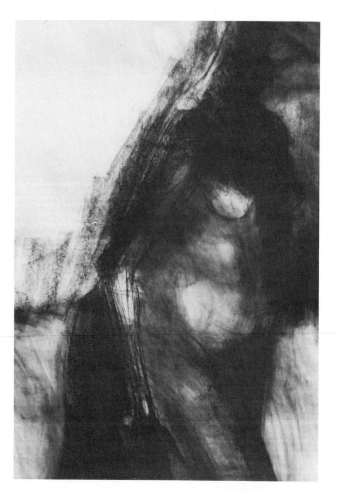

Joseph Gatto, *Figure*, charcoal, 36" x 48" (91.5 x 122 cm)

Much of the quality of representational art depends on the artist's ability to evaluate and utilize properly tonal values. Academies of art, aware of the importance of tone as a visual element, traditionally required students to begin their training by rendering in charcoal, pencil or pen, graphic images of three-dimensional form upon a two-dimensional surface. Although the practice is not now strictly followed, students are generally encouraged to complete exercises in which tone is adopted as the dominant element.

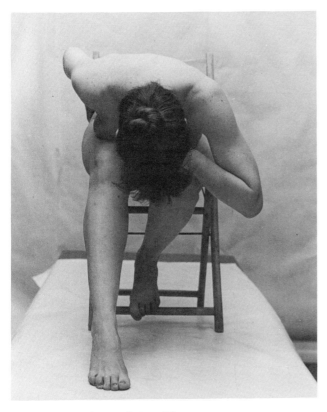

Model with Head Bowed, Front View

Beginning students in tonal drawing exercises show an inherent tendency to *overmodel.* Overmodeling results from the failure to recognize and separate essential tonal values from the abundance of visual information. Essential tonal values position the subject in space relative to the viewer, and establish *placement* of the main projections, prominences and planes of the subject before they are modeled with additional variations of tone.

An exercise that will help the student to avoid overmodeling is demonstrated in the space and tone modeling diagrams. Tone and line are combined into a simplified tonal pattern as a base for establishing and maintaining consistency in representational visual art.

The versatility of tone is increased when coordinated with the element of line. You will realize during the exercise that best results are usually attained when the fewest factors

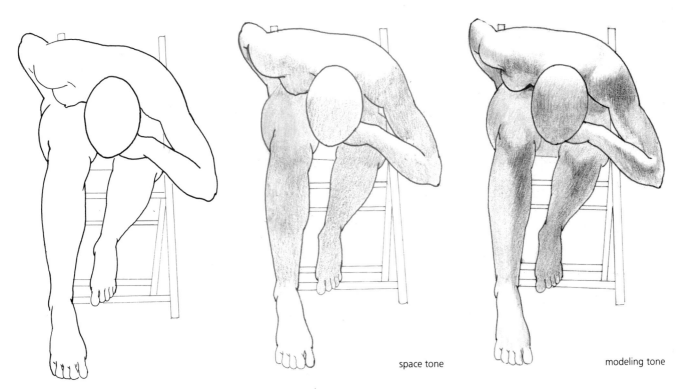

space tone   modeling tone

Space and Tone Modeling Diagrams

are applied to a problem. The objective of the exercise is to demonstrate that a substantial base for a detailed representational drawing can evolve from two closely allied tonal concepts: space tone and modeling tone.

In tonal drawing the subject is conceived through two basic stages. The first employs a value, *space tone,* to place the main structural elements of the subject in their respective spatial locations. The second, *modeling tone,* serves to shape or model the contours and planes of the previously placed structural elements. These stages are analogous to the preparatory phase of a work in sculpture, with clay as the medium and the human figure as the subject. The first stage requires that the roughed-out masses of clay and supporting armature representing the torso and limbs be maneuvered into their proper positions in *space*. In the second stage the planes, contours and accompanying detail can be *modeled* out of the spatially oriented volumes positioned in the first stage.

EXERCISE

Use any dry medium. Either pencil, conte crayon or charcoal is suitable.

1. Following the example demonstrated in the first space and tone modeling diagram sketch with line either the figure in the photograph of the model with the head bowed or a model in the same pose with the same light angle as shown in the photograph.

2. Closely study the photograph or model and compare it with the example showing space tone. You will notice that the planes reflecting most light are equally or similarly placed or angled in space. In this case they are located in the upper contour of the bowed head, the upper contour of the shoulder, the back, and the upper half of the right arm, the upper half of the left forearm, and the right foot. Throughout the exercise the areas representing these planes must remain untouched.

3. Following the space tone example, apply a tone, a few degrees above the middle of the tonal scale, over the entire

figure with the exception of the areas designated to remain untouched in item 2.

4. Following the modeling tone example, begin to model the form by applying a middle tone or slightly darker value near the edges of the previously applied tone where it encounters the light areas of the shoulders, the head, the left planes of the right and left legs, the lower planes of the left and right arms and the total area of the left foot. In the modeling tone diagram the tone has been extended to indicate the lesser planes and facets of the limbs, like the deltoid mass at the left shoulder, the biceps of the left arm and the facets below each knee.

Texture

Texture is the element that contributes sensuality to visual art. Throughout the history of representational painting, drawing and graphics, the remaining elements, line, tone and color, have frequently been employed to imitate the quality of texture. Museums and private collections are well stocked with realistic depictions of fabric and flesh in portraiture, craggy mountainsides and bristling fields in landscapes, the burnished patina of copper and highlighted porcelain in still life. For a long period of time, especially in drawing and painting, visual art was considered a craft in which the ideal goal of the artist was to create an illusion of physical reality while disguising the medium through which it was realized. Eventually painters noticed that the medium itself, notably oil pigment because of its density and viscosity, could retain the vigorous impression of a brushstroke and the metallic impact of a palette knife. Artists then became aware that variations in texture added a physical dimension to a medium, intensifying its expressive potentials. The texture of a medium could be as sensually attractive as the subject it graphically represented.

Rembrandt's paintings, especially his later ones, were underpainted with a light opaque *textured* impasto that complimented the subtle transparent glazes on the surface.

Vincent van Gogh, *The Harvest,* **pencil and brown ink over graphite, 12¹⁄₂″ x 9¹⁄₂″ (32 x 24 cm), National Gallery of Art, Washington, Collection of Mr. and Mrs. Paul Mellon**

The most renowned examples of textural virtuosity are in the art of Vincent van Gogh, physically real in his painting, graphically implied in his drawings. His paintings show the pigment thickly stroked on the canvas with no intention of retouching or blending. His drawings, usually completed with vigorous motions and pressures of a reed pen, seem to be monochromatic rehearsals for intensely colored, textured paintings to be completed later.

As a class experiment an image of van Gogh's drawing *The Harvest* was projected on a screen. At the same time, at the rear of the room, the stroked patterns of its composition were copied with hard chalk on a blackboard. By listening to the varied prolonged and staccato sounds of the chalk upon the hard surface of the blackboard, the students easily identified the areas that were being explored. Texture can be sensed through sound and sight as well as touch.

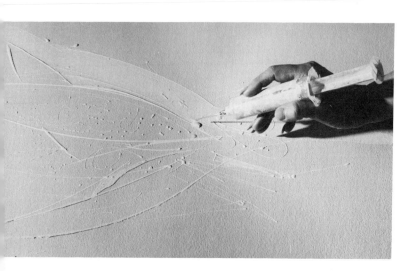

Hand Holding Extruder

Brushstroke Being Applied to Textured Image

Texture Techniques

The varieties of available and acceptable materials for developing texture are innumerable. Sand, chips of glass, wood and even uncooked pasta have been and are still being inserted, sprayed, brushed and splattered into layers of glue, gesso and other viscous substances. Effective combinations are limited only by the artist's imagination, technical proficiency and self-generated guidelines based upon well-proven rules. Keep in mind that texture can impair as well as enhance the quality of visual art. Texture should be used for a definite objective. Too often it is adopted as a surefire way of attracting attention or to disguise ineptness. Texture, when utilized with thoughtfulness, prudence and objectivity, not only adds a tangible dimension to a work of art, it also complements and often intensifies the uniqueness of each of its elements.

A standard method of developing a mixed media work on a textured surface consists of two stages. In the first stage a semiliquid substance is shaped into a basic design, a relief pattern, and allowed to dry. In the next stage the pattern is activated with whatever method or material seems appropriate. Many artists begin by rubbing dry media like charcoal and crayon upon the surface; others may start by using thin washes of ink, watercolor or even oil pigment thinned with turpentine. The choices are limitless.

The use of texture applied in a semiliquid state is demonstrated in the photograph of a hand holding an extruder, which is a hypodermic device used for injecting fillings into pastries. The extruded material is gesso, thinned to the consistency of heavy cream. Gesso has been used for centuries in textured relief underpainting and has proven to be malleable, tough and permanent. Fluid material may also be applied by using squeezable plastic containers or dripping it from palette knives, putty knives, sticks or brushes.

After the gesso has dried, a wash of black ink is *floated* over selected areas of the textured base with a medium-sized brush, as shown in the illustration. The ink wash allows the detailed pattern to contrast sharply against the dark surroundings. Later, other materials may be added.

Joseph Mugnaini, *Baroque with Red Mama,* **mixed media,**
5'2" x 3'10" (157.5 x 117 cm)

The textured gesso pattern in *Baroque with Red Mama* was
developed with a hypodermic extruder. After the required
drying period (approximately three hours) thin washes of
colored ink were brushed over selected areas of the design.
In the final stage, subtle touches of red and black conte
crayon, charcoal and linear markings with a number 5
Speedball pen were applied. After drying for one day the
surface was sprayed with a clear acrylic coating.

Joseph Gatto, *Figures,* ink wash over gesso, 50" x 24" (127 x 61 cm)

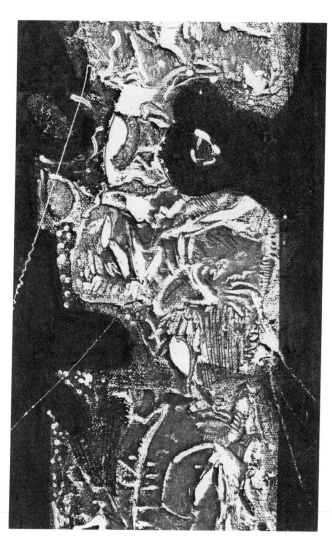

Frania Igloe, untitled, inks over gesso, 5" x 8" (12.5 x 20.5 cm)

The design in *Figures* was completed in a similar manner with one exception. Instead of using a hypodermic extruder, the textured pattern was developed by dripping and brushing gesso onto the surface, then manipulating it, while wet, with the end of a brush and other utensils. After drying, thin washes of colored inks and dry media like charcoal and conte crayon were applied.

The large central shape in Frania Igloe's untitled work was cut out of a sheet of cardboard, pressed into a layer of wet gesso, then suddenly lifted. After drying, the background detail in the main shape was modified and intensified with various colored inks.

Lena del Francia Gibbs, *White Mountain,* **yellow ocher and black oil glazes over white zinc paste, 18" x 24" (46 x 61 cm)**

The first stage of the mountain landscape in *White Mountain* was modeled with zinc paste to resemble low relief sculpture. It is a technique that resembles the textured underpaintings of Rembrandt. The final stage was completed by brushing washes of black, sepia and earth red inks over the total surface and allowing them to sink into the textured crevices, edges and contours of the basic design.

Chapter 3

Media

A youth who likes to study should know that there are six essentials in painting. The first is called *spirit,* the second *rhythm,* the third *thought,* the fourth *scenery,* the fifth *the brush,* and the last is the *ink.*

                                                    Ching Hao

MUCH OF THE AESTHETIC and expressive quality of visual art depends upon the material used, the instrument with which it is applied, and the way in which it is manipulated. In *Crab,* Albert Porter depicted the subject with a felt-tipped marker. In the second picture he interpreted it with a brush and a transparent wash. In both examples the theme is realistic, yet the *sensual* impression of the medium used in each work is as different as the sound of a guitar and a piano playing the same musical composition. The critical stage in drawing takes place at the moment the surface of the picture plane is contacted. At that instant the senses of sight and touch converge at a focal point where techniques, materials and concept become united on the picture plane.

Just as musical instruments are considered extensions of the human voice, the instruments of visual art may be recognized as extensions of the human hand. Visual art is produced by combining the instrument or applicator with the material or medium through the process of drawing or painting upon the surface of the picture plane.

To appreciate fully the importance of the picture plane, consider it as the inactive half of the medium that, when drawn upon, becomes *one* with the material used. Remember that the performance of any medium is significantly affected by the texture, size, dimensions, weight and various other qualities of its support. For example, paper should be purposefully selected. Paper with a smooth or hard surface may be suitable for linear ink drawings but not for ink washes. An absorbent surface may be ideal for charcoal, conte or ink wash, but not for linear pen and ink or calligraphic drawing. Newsprint is adequate (even though it is not permanent) for simple charcoal, conte crayon and pencil studies. An excellent utility paper of fair quality for wash, crayon, charcoal, conte and ink, is printers or etching proof paper. It has the weight and texture that may be freely experimented on. In the following section dealing with materials and tools, the type of paper used should be given careful consideration.

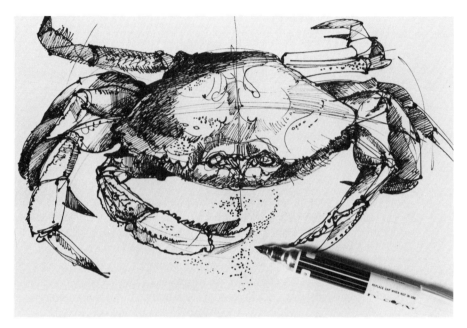

Albert Porter, *Crab,* **felt-tipped pen, 9" x 12" (23 x 30.5 cm)**

Albert Porter, *Crab,* **wash, 9" x 12" (23 x 30.5 cm)**

Holding Chisel-Point Nib Pen

The Pen

The pen is a logical successor to the wedge-tipped stylus originally used to impress hieroglyphic symbols into soft clay. From its origin about 2500 B.C., when it was whittled from reed stalks and later made from the pinion feathers of large birds, the pen has been the principal instrument for transmitting concepts and ideas on parchment and paper. Before the advent of the printing press almost every conceivable human opinion and venture in religion, science, and art was developed and recorded with a pen. The invention of the steel pen in the early nineteenth century made quill and reed pens obsolete. An exception was in the field of visual art where even today both are considered important choices among the various types of ballpoints, fiberglass, felt and steel points available. Regardless of brand name or patented innovations, all pens have nibs that may be classified into several types: rigid, semirigid, flexible, round-pointed, oval-pointed, chisel-pointed and sharp-pointed. A well-known line of pen nibs in which each type is well represented is the Speedball pen available in many sizes.

The nib being demonstrated in the illustration is a Speedball no. 6 chisel-point, a direct descendent of the reed pen. It is especially designed for variations in linear thicknesses. If the point is moved in the direction of its axis, a thin line is derived. When it is moved opposite to its axis, a broad line is realized. Variation in the thickness of line is an important factor in descriptive as well as expressive drawing.

In *Figure Study,* Marie Starr used a no. 6 chisel-point pen to indicate the muscular system and framework of the human body. She stroked in the direction of the nib's axis for the thin line and against its axis for a broad line.

Benjamin Brown used a no. 6 round-point for both the thickly applied curvilinear contour and the thinner, relatively angular internal structure of his *Figure Study*. He increased the weight of the outline by applying pressure with his thumb directly on the nib as it was moved over the surface of the paper.

Marie Starr, *Figure Study,* ink and Speedball pen

Benjamin Brown, *Figure Study,* pen and ink, 16" x 28" (40.5 x 71 cm)

The Pencil

The pencil, like the pen, is extremely adaptable, permanent and universally used. Traditionally referred to as a lead pencil, in reality it is made from a mixture of graphite and refined clay. Like many other items that are easily available and inexpensive, it is too often taken for granted or ignored.

The pencil is one of the most graphically articulate media. In visual art each medium exhibits qualities that distinguish it from others. One can easily determine their uniqueness by testing their performance with the elements line, tone, color and texture.

Line   In developing a pencil drawing you can easily recognize that graphite, being rigid, produces an easily maintained consistent linear thickness. On the other hand, variations in linear markings must be obtained by either sharply rotating the point while it is in motion or using points of varied thickness and shape, such as the carpenter's pencil shown in the illustration.

Joseph Mugnaini, *Alberto Giacometti,* carpenter's pencil and wash, 8¼" x 10" (21 x 25.5 cm)

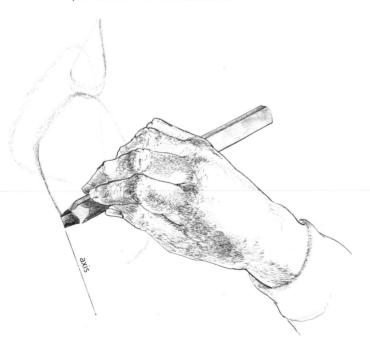

axis

Holding Carpenter's Pencil

Tone   The pencil, as a dry medium, can achieve variation in tone from the most subtle nuances of gray to the deepest dark or absolute black. This range is possible by taking advantage of the various grades of hardness in pencils from 9H, the hardest, to 6B, the softest.

Color   Colored pencils, an increasingly popular medium compounded with a mixture of wax and pigment, can be used to add the dimension of color to a drawing and to correct or redo areas in a watercolor, acrylic and even an oil painting. Although extremely versatile, they nevertheless are subject to the basic limitations and techniques of the graphite pencil. Broad areas of color begin with individual strokes of the tool even though they may be changed to appear as a wash by going over them with a brush and water or paint thinner.

Texture   The texture of graphite is negligible, yet for decades artists have used the pencil to imitate every texture imaginable.

Gretel Stephens, *Figure,* pencil, 18" x 24" (46 x 61 cm)

Edward Reep, *Reclining Figure,* pencil, 18" x 24" (46 x 61 cm)

A pencil that has proven to be an interesting, rewarding alternative to the familiar round-pointed type is the carpenter's pencil, used by woodworkers for accurate measurement. Its rectangular core may be sharpened to a wedge-shaped tip similar to a reed pen. When the stroke is moved in the direction of its bladelike axis, a thin line is produced. A movement opposite to its axis results in a broad line. A looping or arching stroke produces measures of both. An example of the lines produced is shown in the illustration, where the pencil is held in a firm, fixed position.

The portrait *Alberto Giacometti* was drawn with a soft grade carpenter's pencil and a light ink wash. The outlines of the head, collar and the detail of the shirt were completed with the axis of the tip in a vertical and semivertical position. The eyebrows and the structural features of the right side of the head were sketched with the broad side of the tip opposite to the axis. The dark, nearly black strokes indicating the hair mass and color were developed by applying the broadside of the tip in the required areas while the wash was wet.

The drawings by Gretel Stevens and Edward Reep are based on a similar theme, the reclining figure. They are excellent examples of point-to-point contour drawing executed with a pencil. Subtle variations in line are a result of rhythmic strokes stimulated by a knowledge of human anatomy and a familiarity with basic postures assumed by the human figure.

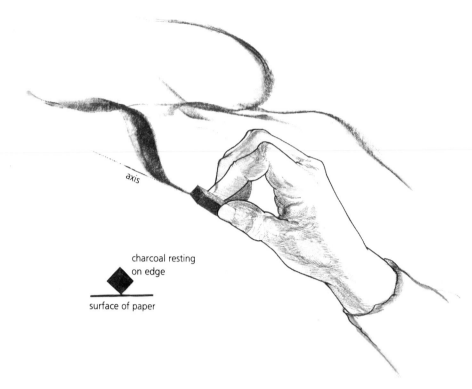

axis

charcoal resting
on edge

surface of paper

Charcoal

The oldest and most widely used dry medium is charcoal. It is available in two varieties: vine or stick charcoal and compressed charcoal. *Stick charcoal* is made from twigs of trees with fine-grained wood. It is sold in either a cylindrical form or in a square, elongated form. It is brittle, soft and must be handled carefully. It works best on textured paper or charcoal paper that is made expressly for it. Easily corrected, it can be made permanent by spraying it with fixatives that are stocked by most art supply stores. *Compressed charcoal* can be used on various surfaces that are not too smooth. Because of its binder it adheres to the surface of the paper and does not necessarily require a fixative. It may be either built up or rubbed to produce the dark, velvety qualities of black that can be achieved with a dry medium. The shape of the compressed charcoal affects its performance. Many artists who use this medium prefer the cylindrical type, but others find the square type provides a variety of ways in which the paper may be sensitively contacted. With skillful manipulation the sides, planes, edges and tips of the charcoal can be maneuvered with varied speeds and pressures to register the expressive potentials of line and tone. An efficient method of gripping a cubelike piece of charcoal to control variations in the thickness of line is illustrated. This method also applies to other media of a similar shape, like crayons, conte, pastels and chalks.

In order to understand and make use of the expressive potentials of a dry medium the following exercise is recommended. You should stand while doing this exercise.

EXERCISE

1. Fix a relatively large sheet of paper on a drawing board and place the board flat on a bench or table.

2. Lay a piece of *cube*-shaped charcoal or conte crayon near the top edge of the paper at arm's length.

3. Hold the charcoal or conte between your thumb and combined index and middle fingers. Tilt it so that the entire length of the bladelike edge is in contact with the surface.

4. Rotate it like the hand of a clock until it is in a vertical position in relation to the paper, or at a right angle to the bottom edge of the paper, and tilt it until its long edge contacts the surface of the paper.

5. Still maintaining the charcoal or crayon in the tilted position shown in the illustration, *pull* it toward you with your arm in an extended, rigid position. You will notice that you have drawn a fairly consistent thin line.

6. Repeat the stroke, except this time move it right and left and in a sweeping arc. The result will be a line of varying thickness. Continued differences in pressure, motion and speed produce infinite variations in the *weight* and thickness of line.

Georges Seurat, *The Embroideress,* **conte crayon, 11³/₁₆" x 9⁵/₁₆" (28.5 x 24 cm), Norton Simon, Inc., Museum of Art, Pasadena**

Richard Lees, *Seated Figure,* **charcoal, 16" x 25" (40.5 x 63.5 cm)**

Georges Seurat, considered to be the principal exponent of *pointillist* painting, was aware of the tonal as well as the chromatic content of color. He knew, for example, that reds, when photographed in black and white, register in the lower range of the tonal scale, while yellows rise to the upper levels. *The Embroideress* is an example from his numerous studies showing the tonal element underlying the chromatic patterns of his designs. It is rendered in black conte crayon, vigorously applied and rubbed into the surface of paper especially textured for crayon and charcoal. The element of line has been subdued, yet it is used to demarcate the lightest area of the design in the lower central region of the picture plane.

In *Seated Figure* rubbing has been restricted. Richard Lees used the bladelike edges, tips and points of conte crayon to produce this drawing. By employing various pressures, speeds and movements with any of the angular-shaped media a skilled draftsperson is able to activate the picture plane like a musician manipulating the keyboard of a piano or fingering the strings of a violin.

Mildred Walker, *I Am So Handsome,* **black chalk, 18" x 24" (46 x 61 cm)**

Black Chalk

Black chalk, like other dry black media, produces a unique textural quality with a rich velvety blackness. Expertly handled, it easily produces values ranging from subtle light grays to deep blacks. Since the Renaissance, artists have applied black chalk to various surfaces, including canvas, wood and plaster as well as paper. Lately it is being recognized as a versatile permanent medium.

The tonal values in *I Am So Handsome* extend the full range of the light-and-dark scale. The light areas in the upper region of the picture plane have been *trapped* and surrounded by darks, while the lower light area has been *invaded* by energetic dark linear thrusts. Mildred Walker rubbed the chalk to produce variations in tone traditionally referred to as chiaroscuro. The image is reminiscent of the satirical etchings of Goya and the iconoclastic lithographs of Daumier.

Walker developed the subject in *Figure Study* in two stages. In the first stage she used a middle tone to produce the tonal pattern indicating the main planes of the head, torso and limbs. Secondary planes, detail and linear contour were modeled with expertly applied strokes of the edges and point of the angular-shaped chalk. Regarding both drawings Walker says:

Topical figure drawing goes beyond the artist's technical performance in that it expresses personal convictions and perception of human nature. I am fascinated with our attempts, sometimes amusing, sometimes pathetic, to deal with life's servings of weal and woe. How Handsome I Am has to do, in general, with our inclination to avoid confronting and admitting our shortcomings. This drawing in particular is a comment on the myopic buffoons who see themselves as paragons of wit and charm.

Nonthematic figure drawings are, in my opinion, far more than studies. While technical quality and style are both products of the artist's skill and intention, they alone cannot give the drawing its own energy. I believe that the dynamics—the power—of figure drawing lies in the

Mildred Walker, *Figure Study*, black chalk, 18" x 24" (46 x 61 cm)

artist's attunement to the abstract rhythms of flow and counterflow, relaxation and tension and the capacity for letting these elements affect the final statement. The drawing is both an intellectual and an emotional exercise.

Conte Crayon

Conte crayon continues to be a popular expressive medium. It too is available in either a cylindrical or cubelike form in four basic colors: black, white, sepia and earth red. Recently grays, earth green, yellow ocher and others have been added. The hardness of conte crayon varies from soft through medium to hard. It is a finely ground chalk with an oil binder and does not necessarily require a fixative.

The unmistakable angular sharp-edged markings of the *cube-shaped* conte crayon are seen in *Head of Woman.* Comments by Harold Frank reveal how the function of the medium is affected by its shape:

A drawing has its own need to be solved in its area of space, line, movement, but not necessarily completely resolved. In this case, working with conte crayon, I used the edges, sides, the longitudinal fullness for utmost variation, here and there inviting a crisp line—not because it was visible in the figure, only because the drawing necessitated it.

The Brush

The instrument most responsive to the sense of touch is the brush. The round watercolor brush, similar to that used in oriental sumi painting, is the most sensitive. The character and quality of a brush drawing depend upon variations in speed, pressure, elevation and movement while the brush is being manipulated. Accents are achieved by suddenly increasing pressure or arresting motion. Thickness is modulated either by elevating or lowering the point during the stroking. Lowering the tool narrows the stroke; elevating it broadens the stroke.

Harold Frank, *Head of Woman,* **conte crayon, 18" x 24 " (46 x 61 cm)**

In *Nude Study*, Sam Clayberger used a quarter-inch pig-bristle oil painting brush to sketch the back of a female figure. The briskly applied hard-edged strokes indicate the brush is blunt-edged and rigid and produces a line of consistent thickness.

In contrast, the symbols in the calligraphic study are of varying weights. The thick-to-thin characteristics show that these markings were produced by either a long-bristled pointed sable brush or an oriental sumi brush. In this case a sumi brush was used.

Anon, calligraphic exercise, sumi brush, 24" x 32" (61 x 81 cm)

Sam Clayberger, *Nude Study*, brush and ink, 18" x 24 " (46 x 61 cm)

Thomas Van Sant, *Joseph Mugnaini,* **diluted ink and brush, 12"**
x 18" (30.5 x 46 cm)

The head by Thomas Van Sant is a combination of a wash
and point-to-point contour drawing. The medium is an
india ink solution of one part ink to three parts water. The
artist used the side of a round watercolor brush as well as
its tip to produce the broad, transparent accents of the
beard and hair.

The point-to-point contour drawing by *Nancy Foote* was
completed with a sumi-type brush. By scanning the image,
one can review its development through a succession of
sensitively applied staccato strokes of a pointed brush loaded
with ink, elevated and lowered in rhythmic sequences at
varying speeds.

Nancy Foote, *Seated Figure,* **brush and ink, 16" x 20" (40.5 x**
51 cm)

Gail Lindstrom, *Mountainscape,* **ink washes on rice paper, 10¹⁄₂" x 4¹⁄₄" (26.5 x 11 cm)**

The ink wash drawing by Gail Lindstrom was rendered with a sumi brush on white rice paper. Many of the linear patterns and accents were softened by inserting them into areas that were partially dampened, especially in the upper area of the picture plane where the summit of the mountain merges with the sky. The rice paper support is ideally receptive to transparent and opaque washes.

Sam Clayberger's *Park Benches* is an example of balanced spatial organization. The lower part, dominated by a white tonal area, is accented with freely applied brushstrokes comparable to the calligraphy study shown earlier. In contrast, the artist reduced the upper region to an intricate white pattern representing the trunks, branches and limbs of trees by deliberately filling with black the spaces between them.

Sam Clayberger, *Park Benches,* **brush and ink, 12" x 15" (30.5 x 38 cm)**

Albert Porter, *Silhouette*, brush and ink, 9" x 5" (23 x 12.5 cm)

Sam Clayberger, *Kneeling Figure*, brush and ink, 10" x 15" (25.5 x 38 cm)

The unique quality of a well-conceived, skillfully rendered wash drawing or painting, whether it is in watercolor or ink, is mainly due to a permanent appearance of transparent wetness recorded with freely maneuvered brushstrokes of a liquid medium. Regardless of how long ago the wash drawing was completed, the lasting impression of *wetness* is an intrinsic element of its design. The fresh, transparent clarity of ink and wash drawings by Leonardo da Vinci, Michelangelo, Rembrandt and many contemporary artists often are as impressive as the work for which they served as studies.

Vignette sketches, images isolated within the untouched area of the picture plane, were developed in two stages in *Silhouette* and *Kneeling Figure.* In the initial stage the main shapes were blocked out with extrawet dark washes. In the second and final stage the residual puddles of the first stage were brushed with added ink toward the borders of the image and beyond to indicate the protruding masts and superstructure of the vessel and the hair mass and limbs of the figure. In both drawings, the spontaneous, fresh wet quality of a dark wash is permanently impressed into the fiber of the paper. Vigorous strokes of the brush in both drawings are comparable to the calligraphic symbols we saw earlier in the chapter.

Rieta Jones, *Music Man,* wash drawing, oil on paper, 12" x 18" (30.5 x 46 cm)

The wash drawing *Music Man,* by Rieta Jones, demonstrates that there is no definite separation between expressive drawing and painting. The artist completed the drawing on paper with black oil pigment. Working with oils on paper is not unusual. For centuries artists have used paper as well as wood and canvas for a support.

By reducing the consistency of any liquid or semiliquid medium, the artist is able to introduce one of the most important elements of visual art, the quality of transparency, into his or her design. Each medium has its solvent: turpentine, or a substitute, for oils; water for acrylics, tempera, watercolor and inks. Dry media like charcoal, conte crayon, graphite pencils and pastels may also be blended or modified either with water or an oil solvent.

Rico LeBrun, *Figures from the Flood,* **wash and ink, 14" x 16"
(35.5 x 40.5 cm), Collection of Joseph Gatto**

In *Figures from the Flood* two shapes were initially *trapped from the outside* with a middle tone ink wash, then completed with free calligraphic pen line. The heavy strokes shown in the left upper thigh of the figure on the left were dragged in from the surrounding wash before it dried. The artist used a no. 6 chisel-point Speedball pen tip.

Sharon Falk, *Falcon,* **wash, 10" x 12" (25.5 x 30.5 cm)**

Falcon is another example of the vignette, an image isolated and surrounded by the untouched area of the picture plane. The fresh-appearing passages of tone in the wings and tail were realized in two stages. First the artist indicated a general pattern of the subject with light semiwet washes. Then she deftly administered accents while the first stage was still damp.

In *Figure Study* a point-to-point pen and ink contour draw-ing was quickly incised into a light, damp wash. This proce-dure created subtle tones that suggest the surface planes and volumes of the human figure.

The elements of line and tone have been employed with minimum effort and maximum effect in two drawings by Jirayr Zorthian. A basic middle tone pattern of the wash drawing *Gibbons* was first indicated with a few expertly calculated strokes applied with the sides of a round water-color brush. The final state was consummated with calli-graphic strokes of a darker wash applied with the tip of the brush.

The artist completed the contour drawing of a sleeping puppy with a Radiograph pen, a technical pen used in architectural and mechanical drafting. It produces a con-stant line of equal thickness. The general contour of the image was done with a continuous motion, except for sev-eral anatomical features that required detail.

Edward Reep, *Figure Study,* ink and wash, 18" x 24" (46 x 61 cm)

Jirayr Zorthian, *Red Bone Fox Hound,* pen and ink, 5" x 8" (12.5 x 20.5 cm)

Jirayr Zorthian, *Gibbons,* **ink wash, 10" x 15" (25.5 x 38 cm)**

Meredith Olson, *Rain Grass,* **brush and ink, 26" x 40" (66 x 101.5 cm)**

The methods for achieving special effects in visual art are limitless. Many are realized by manipulating or processing traditionally approved materials through unorthodox methods. A description of the unconventional approach used in *Rain Grass* is offered by Meredith Ann Olson, the artist:

Watercolor paper was placed on a flat masonite panel. The poured ink *method was used to establish the basic patterns of design. Black ink was poured directly from the bottle and lighter values from separate containers. The flow of the ink was directed by tilting the masonite panel. Lines were incised with a painting knife, and areas blended with a one-inch flat ox-hair brush. The paper and ink were allowed to dry thoroughly to permit the ink to set. The paper was again presoaked. While the paper was under water, areas could be lightened by rubbing gently with the hand or a soft-bristle brush. The grass was achieved by the sgraffito technique of scratching through the darker ink areas to expose the lighter paper. The repeated scratching was made by using a heavy-grained sandpaper and a razor blade. The final value modulations were made with ink washes using a half-inch flat ox-hair brush.*

Marilyn Kemppaninen, *Winter Rose*, ink, enamel, rose petal, gold leaf on paper, 45" x 47" (114.5 x 119.5 cm)

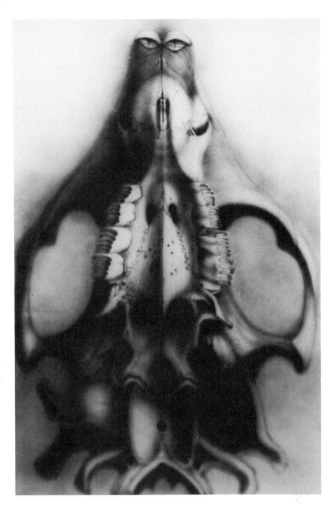

Robert Weaver, *Megamorphosis I*, airbrush, 24" x 36" (61 x 91.5 cm)

A drawing may be conceived and realized through an infinite number of methods and materials. Limitations are set by prudence, a sense of aesthetics and sound crafts-manship. Marilyn Kemppainen comments on her *Winter Rose,* which, with little doubt, is not a typical example of mixed media:

Working direct, the image was made by spraying ink from plastic spray bottles for plants, and spraying enamel paint over rose canes and rose petals on paper. Dried and flat-tened rose petals and composition metal leaf were collaged to it. The lines were made with sticks, pen point and brush. The rose bush in its dormancy is as fascinating to me as one in bloom; the thorns are as intriguing as the petals. The intention is to create a visual metaphor that has several implications by contrasting the dormant, dark and sharp with movement, light and softness. The rose bush is dor-mant and yet there is the memory of the rose. A gust of wind and the petals are dispersed. Time and seasonal change are implied. With the isolation/desolation of the rose bush and the remnants of an afterimage, this drawing has a bit of an ominous note, perhaps a premonition of a future winter.

The Airbrush

The airbrush is one of the most effective instruments for controlling liquid media. Beginning around the middle of this century, it was adopted by countless artists in almost every known field of visual art, especially in the areas of illustration and advertising. The airbrush is unequaled as an instrument for achieving subtle transitions of tone and refined variations in color, yet, like all instruments, it has its limitations. Sharply defined detail in an airbrush drawing normally is developed only through the use of stencils that must be carefully applied to the surface before spraying. This is why Robert Weaver's drawing, which was com-pleted without stencils, is a remarkable achievement. He created the volumes, planes and intricate detail by using various speeds and elevations while maneuvering the air-brush.

The Blade

Experimenting with a wide wedge-shaped instrument serves at least two purposes. First, it helps you to sense and understand what is meant by *pulling a line*. The experience may be applied to help control the element of line with other instruments such as the pencil, pen and brush, especially in the maintenance of consistency and rhythm in contour drawing. Second, the mental discipline and physical coordination required to maneuver the inflexible blade serve to establish a liaison between the visual and tactile senses.

Holding a Putty Knife

EXERCISE

Equipment: An ordinary putty knife that can be purchased at a hardware store; india ink in a wide-mouthed container; a sturdy sheet of paper at least 18" x 24" (46 x 61 cm) in size; a smooth-surfaced drawing board.

1. Fasten the paper firmly to the drawing board and lay it flat on a table or an adjustable easel.

2. Work from a standing position. This helps to involve the body as well as the arms and hand in what may be truthfully referred to as an *act* of drawing in which the physical sense of contact assumes priority over the sense of sight.

3. After dipping the blade into the container of ink, hold it at arm's length. Place its axis, the long edge, at a twelve o'clock position, vertical or perpendicular to the bottom edge of the paper. Leaning back on your heels, with one arm extended, pull the blade toward yourself. The motion is illustrated in the photograph.

4. Try it again, but this time move the blade laterally as well as vertically. You will notice that as with the reed pen, the chisel-point Speedball and the carpenter's pencil, a motion in the direction of the axis of the blade produces a thin line while a movement opposite to its axis forms a broad line.

The subject in the figure demonstrating a bladestroke in a partially completed drawing is a rocky outcropping in Death Valley, California. The heavy markings were produced with the broad end of the blade, the linear impressions with the thin *skating* edge. The short staccato strokes were actually *stamped* on the surface of the paper by a series of repeated tappings of the tip held in a vertical position.

The horizontal detail in the next illustration also was stamped on the surface. In this case, however, a slight lateral movement was added, creating a slicing effect. The blacks were produced by the broad edge loaded with ink. Other liquid media such as watercolor, diluted oils, acrylics and colored inks also may be used for blade work.

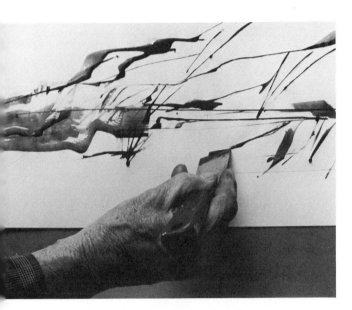

Demonstrating Bladestroke Midway through a Drawing

Drawing Being Completed, Hand and Blade Shown

Completed Drawing

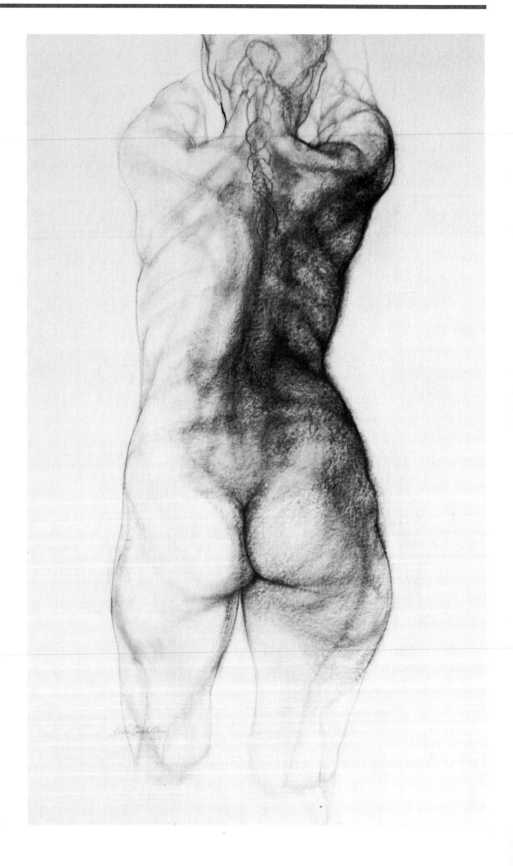

Adrian van Suchtelen, *Back of Female Figure,* **black conte crayon, 25" x 35" (63.5 x 89 cm)**

Part 2

The Practice

IN VISUAL ART the term *technique* refers to the method by which the artist effectively merges concept and medium into a personal idiom or style. It is how the artist exploits potentials while avoiding personal limitations. Traditionally, experiments with various styles have proven helpful in directing the student toward an awareness of her or his own potentials. Paradoxically, however, the student of today can be overwhelmed by the many modern methods of reproduction and distribution. The responsibility of art education today is to provide students with the means to combine the practical and comprehensible aspects of visual art into a personal, expressive idiom generally recognized as a technique or style.

The following chapters address the problem by reducing the mass of available material to fundamental perceptual and conceptual factors that both traditional and contemporary art have in common. The result is presented through seven drawing concepts, two of which—*schematic* and *extended form drawing*—are meant to acquaint the student with the principles of draftsmanship. The remaining concepts—*contour drawing, contained form drawing, calligraphic drawing, action drawing* and *crosshatch drawing*—are approaches to aesthetic and creative expression. They will be discussed and demonstrated following the chapter on design.

The text and exercises presented in the next chapters, beginning with schematic drawing, will introduce methods designed to probe, with the element of line, the intrinsic nature of form and the principles that determine its structure.

Chapter 4

Schematic

Drawing

See the dog before the fleas.
Drawing class credo

S CHEMATIC DRAWING is based on a concept through which the apparent complexity of an object, subject or visual phenomena may be "broken down" into graphic simplicity. A mathematical analogy would be reducing the fraction five-hundred thousandths (500/1000) to one-half ($^1/_2$). The equivalent result is represented by two digits instead of seven. The opposite of schematic drawing is exemplified in the elaborate imagery and rich detail of baroque art. The distinct styles of baroque art and the other movements are derived from either an embellishment or a systematic simplification of structural factors. These factors, which are manifestations of the inseparable relationship between function and form, can be detected and diagramed through schematic drawing.

In drawing we learn about an object or an event by comparing it to others of a similar nature. The objective is to find the common denominator that determines the basic function and shape of each subject that is being analyzed. The essential factors, which are usually hidden or disguised, may be detected by logical observation and elimination of excessive detail.

The simplification procedure is shown in the figure in which a baroque bottle is reduced to its functional shape. A logical appraisal of the bottle reveals that, regardless of its ornate design, it is primarily a container for liquids. Notice that its upper region has been constricted to control the flow of the contents when poured from the opening. The essential structural scheme of a bottle is a combination of container and funnel. Its functional shape is symbolized by a large rectangle to represent the container, and by a triangle topped by a smaller rectangle to represent the funnel.

The shape of a pear has been chosen to represent organic form in general, and the human figure in particular. The variations in its mass, its fairly consistent symmetry and its curvilinear profile provide a basic model for illustrating concepts, techniques and personal imagery. In the drawing the pear is interpreted through schematic drawing in two stages. The normal appearance of the subject is reduced to a simple, almost geometric equation through *schematic* drawing in the first stage. In the second and final stage the

Baroque Bottle and Functional Shape

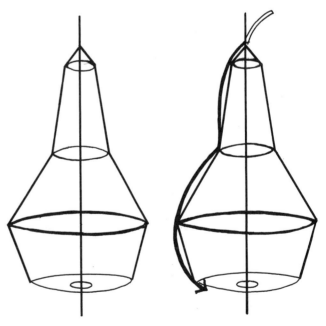

Schematic Drawing of a Pear

drawing is completed with a cursive arching line that rebounds from the angular planes designated by the schematic diagram. The arching linear contour represents mass being *added* to the basic planes of the subject.

Pears in the Styles of Rubens and El Greco

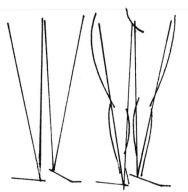

Three indispensable components of visual art are consistency, harmony and rhythm. When specific elements, areas or segments of a drawing are out of proportion they are essentially out of rhythm. Their cadence is inconsistent, incomplete or annoyingly interrupted. If we keep this in mind, the term distortion will be reevaluated and the poetic license or graphic metaphors recognized in the imagery of artists such as El Greco and Rubens will be understood. Schematic drawing will help to maintain consistency and harmony in a work of art regardless of style.

The rotund style of Peter Paul Rubens and the elongated image of El Greco, two distinctly different styles, are nevertheless founded upon structural principles just demonstrated. Next to each figure in the drawing showing their styles, a hypothetical version of a pear is depicted as it would be conceived by both artists. Below each silhouette, the lower limbs have been *schematized* to conform to the style of each artist. Consistency is evident in both examples.

Schematic drawing is a proven approach toward developing *selective vision*. It is a logical method of visualizing hidden essentials within a subject that are usually masked by outward appearance. A schematic analysis of form is conducted simply. The objective is to reduce or eliminate the superfluous contours and unessential detail of an object to a point where further reduction would affect its function and, consequently, its appearance (shape).

The essence of a subject can be isolated and graphically symbolized through careful observation and logical appraisal. The procedure as applied to an event is illustrated in the drawing of a wave striking a rock. Knowing that function and shape are inseparable, we can assume that the outward appearance of a subject or the visible progression of an event, like a wave striking a rock, provides clues to the hidden factors that determine both function and shape. In the drawing the arrow is a symbol for the motion of a wave (momentum), the rectangle represents a rock (inertia). In the middle diagram the wave striking the rock is momentarily arrested and its momentum is partially reversed. Enough forward motion is maintained,

however, to form an arc over the rock, as shown in the lower diagram. The *anatomy* of a wave, manifested through the media of wind and water, can be detected by selective vision and diagramed through schematic drawing.

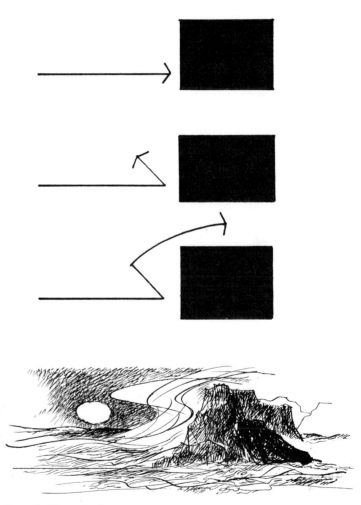

Wave Striking a Rock

Function and Shape

The basic framework of vertebrate life, from the earliest primitive types to present forms, is represented in the composite diagram. It is a neutral abstraction of the spinal column, the pelvic and thoracic girdles, the limbs, the *plates* of the head and the gill bars or jaws. It may be compared to the musical scale, which though limited in range, allows the composer unlimited combinations for musical composition. By repositioning two key elements, the pelvic and thoracic girdles, along the spinal column, nature can vary the vertebrate structure from sardine to shark, mouse to elephant and in the primates, lemur to human.
The strategic location of the pelvic and thoracic girdles is determined by their function. They serve as the *bottom* and *top* of the body cavity (torso) and as anchor for the limbs. Specialization in the vertebrate structure is attained by lengthening or shortening the spinal column and modifying the limbs and head for specific functions.

Regardless of specialization, all vertebrates are endowed with the essential equipment for survival within the limitations of their physical environment. The result is that, in each case, function and shape are interrelated. An appraisal of an animal's essential needs, its size, its method of locomotion and its environment will show that its survival as well as its shape depend on the mechanical design of the vertebrate frame. Its structure must be designed to resist gravity, provide efficient locomotion, protect the vital organs, and promote maneuverability. This includes the adaptation of the limbs or their equivalent, the head and the neck as a tool or weapon. If the horse cannot reach the fly on its back with its mouth it will do so with its tail. These factors reveal clues that help the student artist to develop his or her own *graphic code* through which the apparent complexity of all vertebrates, including humans, may be effectively reintepreted and simplified through schematic drawing.

The diagram of various animal limbs demonstrates how two structural units found in the majority of vertebrates have been modified for a specific function. The examples are the ulna, radius and humerus located in the forelimbs of a cat, the wings of a bird, the flippers of a whale and the wings of a bat.

The cat, the horse and the bird have been chosen to illustrate this structural modification. Using a simple code, their general appearance has been reduced to the structural elements that govern their function as well as their shape. Each animal's form is schematically diagramed with

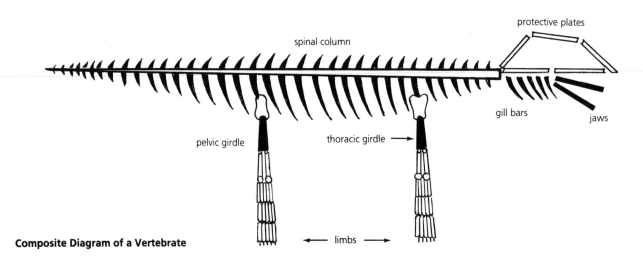

Composite Diagram of a Vertebrate

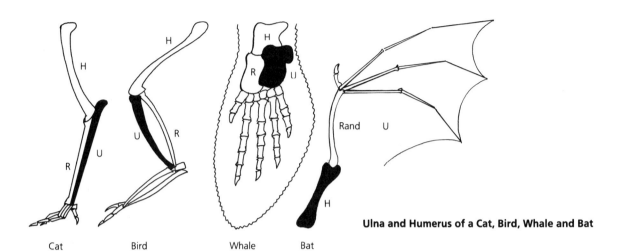

Ulna and Humerus of a Cat, Bird, Whale and Bat

Cat   Bird   Whale   Bat

straight thrusting lines to symbolize spine and limbs and either half or complete ellipses to represent the head and pelvic and thoracic girdles. Top and side views are represented in the drawings.

The cat is an agile, springing type of animal. Its spinal column is well articulated between the widely separated pelvic and thoracic girdles. Because of its universal maneuverability, it does not require a long neck. The head and the limbs are both weapons and tools.

In contrast, the horse, a long-distance runner, requires a semirigid frame. Its pelvic and thoracic girdles are closer together than the cat's. Its limbs are lengthened for speed. The horse must reach food on the ground while in a standing position, so its neck is also lengthened. Its forelimbs and head are both weapons and tools.

The bird's forelimbs have been modified for flight. Its body cavity, aerodynamically designed, is a rigid, overlapping fused combination of the spine and both girdles, pelvic and thoracic. The legs and the combined head and neck are both weapons and tools.

EXERCISE

Break down to a simple graphic equation several forms of animal structure. Select animals that through specialization have developed radical modifications of the basic prototype pattern of a vertebrate. Possible choices would be the frog, turtle and fish.

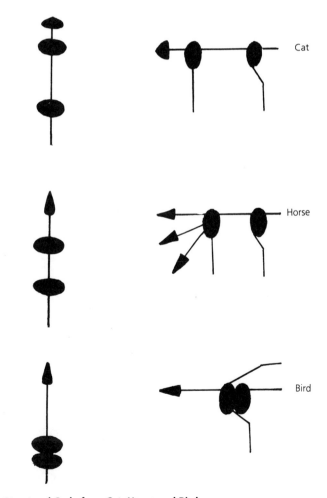

Cat

Horse

Bird

Structural Code for a Cat, Horse and Bird

The Human Figure

Sculptor Henry Moore has stated, "The human form has always been my main concern. It's what we know most about—the softness and slackness of flesh, the hardness of bone, all the energy that is pent up in our bodies. The early Greeks understood that and it came from their deep understanding and close observation of the human figure."

The human figure, undraped or clothed, personalized in portraiture or symbolized in prehistoric artifacts, has been and will continue to be a dominant subject in all art. Since the Willendorf Venus and others like it were carved in stone around 25,000 B.C., the structure of the human body has been studied and its image progressively refined. During the Hellenic period its symmetry and proportions were idealized into the forms that have since been traditionally referred to as "classic." The idealized versions were adopted by the Romans but generally ignored during the Dark Ages, only to be revived during the Renaissance. Since then they have served as aesthetic standards for figurative art and as *models* for figure drawing until the early years of this century.

Current attitude toward drawing from the human figure is positive. Life drawing is a requirement in most art schools and colleges, although the objective is not to emulate the classical examples of the past. Plaster cast copies of antique sculpture are becoming extinct. Still life problems planned as preparatory exercises before drawing from plaster casts are no longer required. Today, the student soon confronts the challenging problem of drawing from a living model. Arguments for and against drawing from life without previous experience should not affect the self-motivated student. Drawing directly from life parallels the experience of artists who have consistently recommended nature as the best teacher.

Aside from a natural interest in the human image, drawing the human figure remains important because it embodies the basic principles of both the visual and plastic arts: functional design and harmonious integration of its components.

In this section the human figure represents not only itself as a subject but also organic structure in general. In addition, it exemplifies efficient composition at the root of aesthetic design. To sense the graceful symmetry of the human figure, one should apply the same objectivity to the model as to the study of the elaborately shaped baroque bottle and the wave striking a rock (both illustrated at the beginning of the chapter).

Hidden causes that determine the shape of a subject can be detected by searching for common factors shared with similar objects. The uniqueness of the human body as a precisely balanced structure is especially noticeable in a standing posture. An erect human figure adjusts itself to the force of gravity with a single vertical line of resistance, as illustrated in the diagrams of lines of resistance. In comparison, most vertebrates (diagram of the quadraped) resist gravity with two lines of resistance, a system comparable to the post and lintel method in architecture—a beam supported by two columns—or the suspension system in engineering—a cable extended between two columns. The human spatial design also can be compared to the architecture of a Gothic cathedral planned to resist gravity with a direct vertical thrust. The lateral projections or movements in the structure of the cathedral must be compensated by either an arch, vault or buttress. Comparably, the human body in an upright position compensates the slightest shift of weight from its central line of resistance with a precisely balanced readjustment that involves its total structure. The human figure, regardless of its posture, is an ideal model, not necessarily to be imitated for its own sake, but as an example of harmony, integrity and purposeful design.

There are other vertebrates that walk and stand on two legs, birds, for example. However, their body framework, being aerodynamically constructed for flight, is rigid and not as articulated as that of the human. Their bodies are cantilevered over a single line of resistance as shown in the diagram. No skillful rendering of feathered detail can make up for a concept that ignores the principle of the cantilever symbolized and schematized in the diagram.

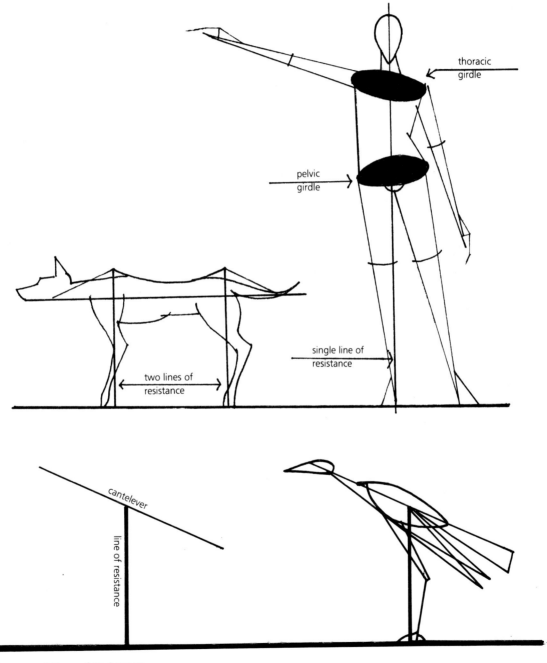

Diagrams of Lines of Resistance

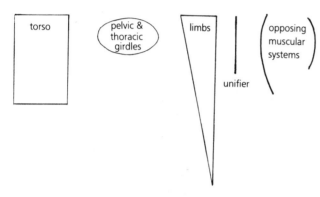

Graphic Alphabet

torso

pelvic & thoracic girdles

limbs

unifier

opposing muscular systems

As an introduction to the practice of schematic drawing, a *graphic alphabet* has proven to be especially effective in analyzing the human figure and vertebrate structure in general. It may also be modified for other subjects. The alphabet consists of six symbols: a rectangle, a triangle, an ellipse or oval, a relatively short straight line, a long arc, and a short arc. In the diagram of the graphic alphabet the rectangle represents the body cavity or torso; the ellipse symbolizes both the pelvic structure (pelvic girdle) and the thoracic assembly (thoracic girdle); the triangle represents the arms and legs; the short thrusting line serves as a unifying element wherever it is required; the long arc and the short arc represent the opposing muscular systems that motivate the limbs.

The basic scheme of the human figure in a standing position with an upraised arm is shown diagramed with the schematic alphabet. In the figure on the right the thrusting lines extending at an angle from the rectangle representing the torso to the base of the arms, describe the outer edge

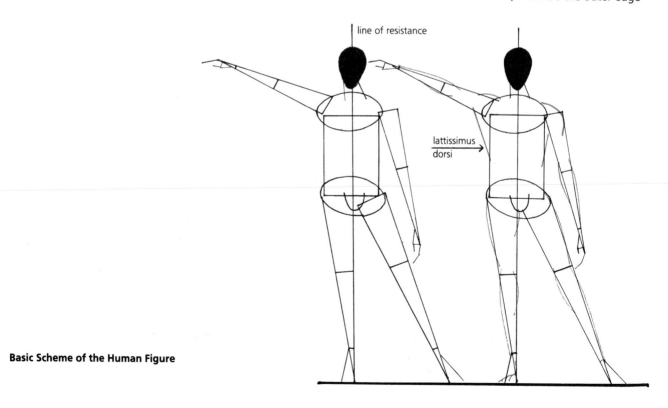

line of resistance

lattissimus dorsi

Basic Scheme of the Human Figure

of the lattisimus dorsi muscular systems that contribute to the triangular appearance of the upper region of the torso. Sharp thrusting lines also indicate the joints that separate the limbs into three segments, the upper arm, forearm and hand, and the thigh, leg and foot. The right side of the figure is contoured with a minimal application of the long and short arcs.

The graphic alphabet may be modified for specific subjects. Consider the schematic drawing of the femur. Part *a* is a medical illustration of the human femur. In *b* the tubular shaft of the femur has been indicated with a lengthened rectangle. The condyle or lower extreme is depicted by a triangle and two small overlapping rectangles. The upper extreme has been indicated with an equilateral triangle, a rectangle and half of an ellipse. In *c* the angular schematic concept is contoured with long and short arcs.

EXERCISE

As an experiment, cut a triangle out of cardboard, proportioned like the one in the diagram of a quadruped. Section it into four segments. By separating the segments and placing them at proper angles, you will be able to depict the basic structural arrangement of the front and rear limbs of most vertebrate quadrupeds. The common denominator is the triangle, a modified two-dimensional version of a cone. The example in the diagram is a schematic concept applied to a member of the canine family.

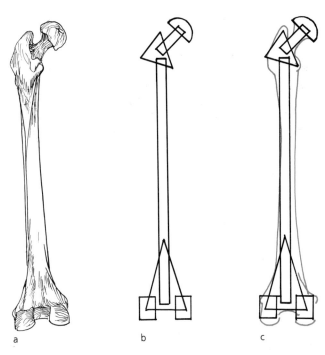

a   b   c

Schematic Drawing of the Femur

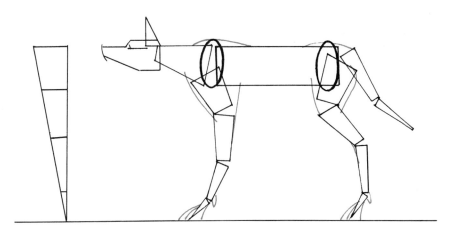

Diagram of a Quadrupeds

The diagrams in this section are derived from blackboard demonstrations and need minimal explanation. They are visual aids to help the student-artist recognize and utilize the harmony and basic simplicity evident in the structure of the human figure. For those who want to explore human anatomy further, the diagrams will serve as schematic patterns to help simplify the apparent complexity of the muscular system and the skeletal framework of the human body.

The uniqueness of the human figure is best displayed when its skeletal and muscular systems are extended to the limit as shown in the photograph. The following diagrams are based upon this extended pose.

The silhouette of the model in an extended pose may be interpreted as the first stage of selective vision that ignores confusing detail. The diagram next to the silhouette demonstrates how the human body can be symbolized by superimposing an X over a rectangle.

The diagram demonstrating the mechanical principle of the *lever* indicates how it is manifested in the body. The lever is apparent in the humerus, ulna and radius of the arm, and the femur, tibia and fibula of the leg. A section of a limb (a) that could be a thigh, leg, upper arm, or forearm is symbolized by a two-dimensional version of the conical structure of the human limb, a triangle. It is flanked by two opposing arcs, one long and shallow, the other short and deep. The arcs indicate the adductor and abductor muscular systems that move the limbs. The triangle flange-shaped scapula (b) is designed as an anchorage and connecting point for the muscles of the back, neck and arms. Diagram c shows that the arms and legs are basically similar in structure, extension and bulk, when viewed in totality from their source, the pelvis, to their terminus; the hands and feet.

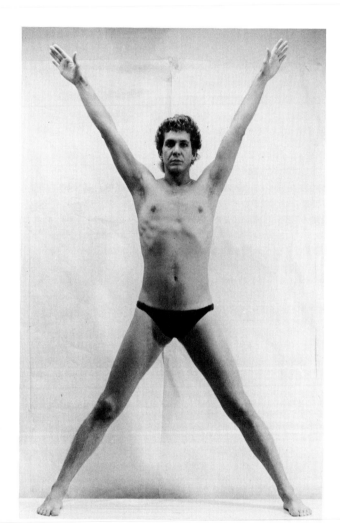

Model in Extended Pose

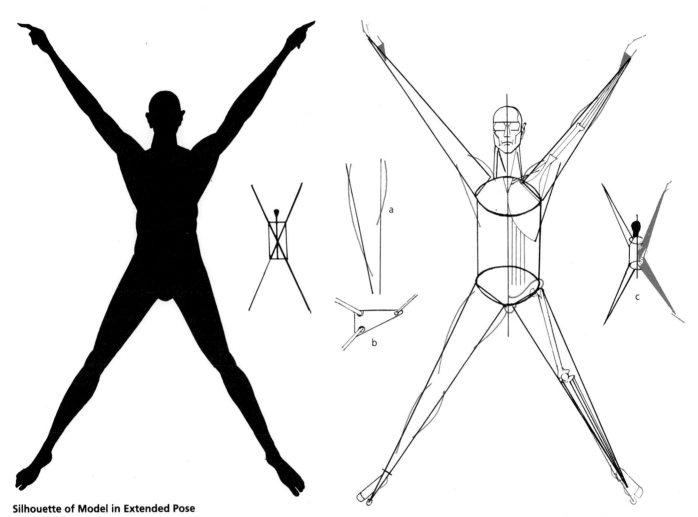

Silhouette of Model in Extended Pose

Diagram Demonstrating the Mechanical Principles of the Lever

The extended figure in profile demonstrates the upward thrust of the arms contrasting with the downward pressure of the legs. The division begins at the pelvis.

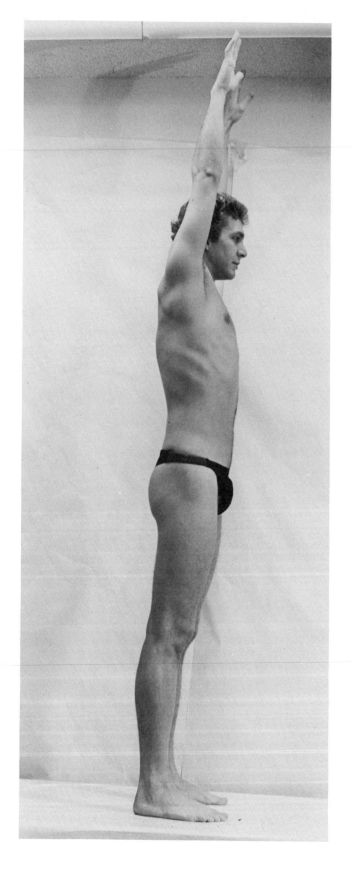

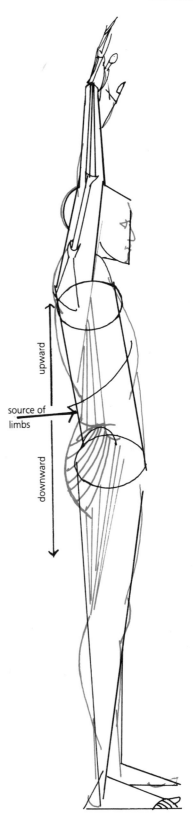

upward

source of
limbs

downward

Extended Figure in Profile

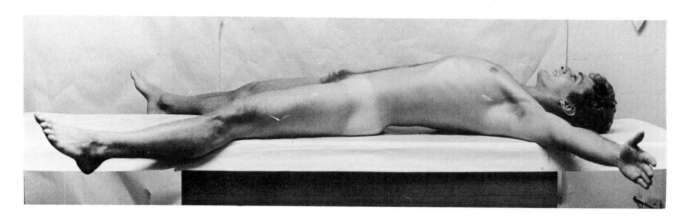

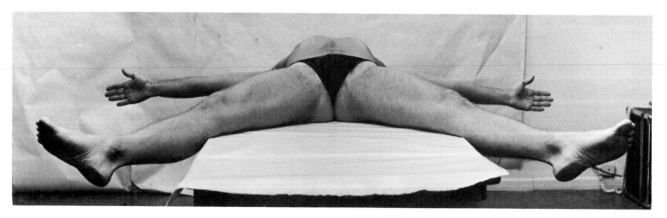

Extended Pose in Reclining Positions

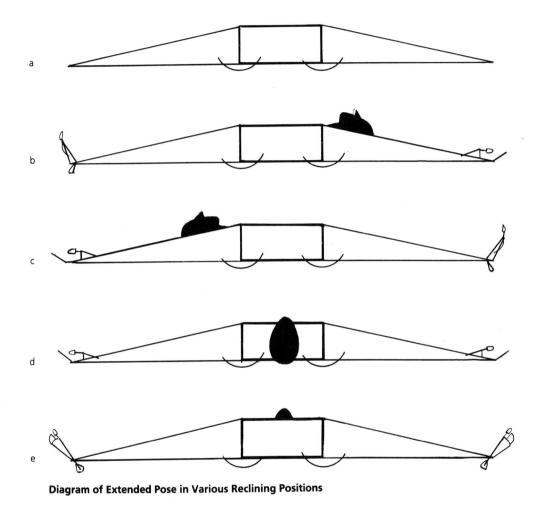

Diagram of Extended Pose in Various Reclining Positions

The extended pose in a reclining position, viewed from various opposing angles, usually presents problems related to *foreshortening*. The apparently complex views can be simplified through schematic drawing.

In the schematic diagrams of the extended reclining figure, the basic concept of the human figure is diagramed with a rectangle to represent the body cavity and triangles to represent the limbs (*a*). The triangular symbol on the right in *b* becomes an arm when the head is located near its base. Reversing the position of the head (*c*) changes the arm to a leg. Placing the head in the middle of the rectangle (*d*) changes the triangles to the arms. Placing the head beyond the rectangle (*e*) identifies the triangles as legs.

Overlapping the thoracic and pelvic girdles foreshortens the torso, as indicated by the model and the diagram. Notice how the thoracic girdle has rotated in comparison to the stable position of the pelvic girdle.

The study of a reclining figure has been schematically diagramed to show how the positioning at the pelvic and thoracic girdles determine the foreshortening of a reclining figure.

Photo and Diagram of Model with Foreshortened Torso

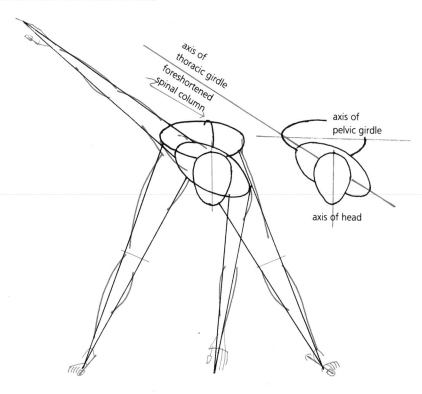

Adrian van Suchtelen, *Reclining Figure,* **conte crayon, 24" x 35"**
(61 x 89 cm), with diagram

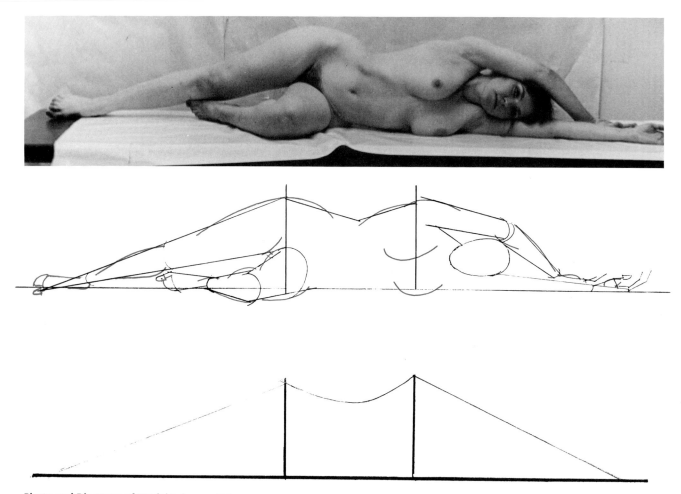

Photo and Diagrams of Model Lying on Side

The human figure lying on its side in an extended position adjusts itself, like a suspension bridge, to the force of gravity. In this case the pelvic and thoracic girdles serve as columns that support the spinal column and muscular systems suspended between them.

One of the priorities of draftsmanship is the ability to resist drawing the enticing, often disconcerting edges or contours of form before they are properly evaluated. This is particularly critical with a subject as complex as the human figure. For decades students have been reminded that *all*

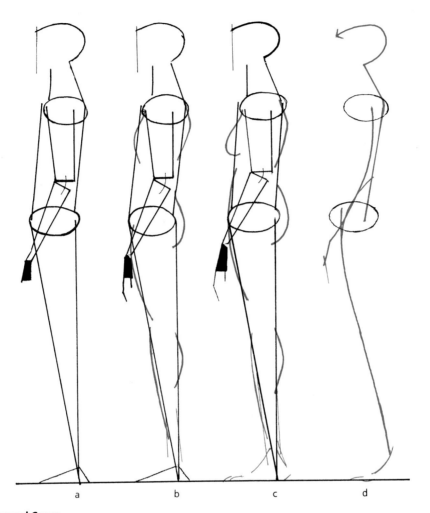

Diagram of Inner Compound Curve

curves are hung from a line, a line being perceived as a graphic definition of the edge of a plane, or the apparent boundary separating the subject from space. Freedom from a normal obsession with outlines and curves is gained by *temporarily* ignoring the attention-monopolizing exterior curvature that distracts the viewer from physical reality.

The diagram of the *inner compound curve* demonstrates how the graceful subtlety of the human figure in profile is dependent upon this. In part *a* the typical human figure is drawn schematically in a standing profile. Even at this early stage, the "hidden" curve has been indicated by the varied positions of the structural elements of the figure. The

"formula" is simple. The primary factors that determine the human figure in this posture are the dorsal (toward the rear) slant of its upper region (torso) and the slope of the frontal plane of the leg toward the vertical line of resistance. In *b* the angular schematic concept is "contoured" with several arcs, some short, some long, to represent the muscular system of the male figure. A slight variation in the arcs depicts the female figure in *c*. The hidden curve is visualized in *d* as it rises from the foot and, reversing its direction, curves through the pelvis and continues upward toward the thoracic girdle, terminating in the head. The added cursive arc symbolizes the head in that position.

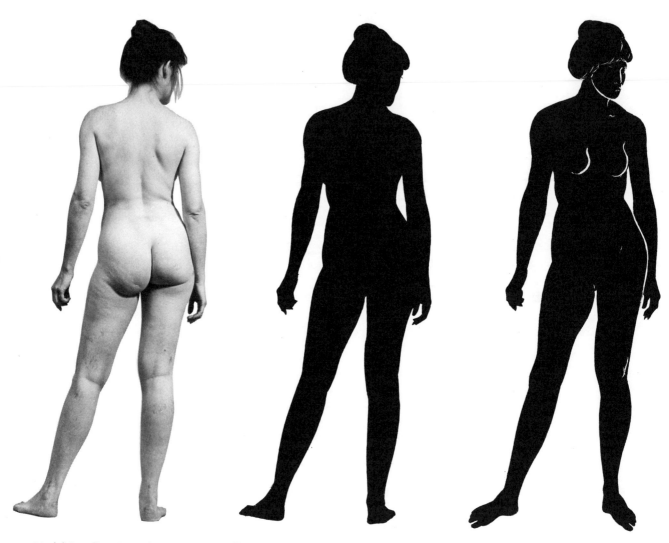

Model Standing, Rear View   **Silhouettes of Standing Model**

The model in the rear view photograph has assumed the most common and most comfortable of human postures while in a standing position. It exemplifies the adaptability and stability of the human body. Equilibrium is maintained by continuous readjustment and control of muscular tension coordinated with a precisely balanced, well-articulated skeletal framework. With few variations it is a pose that has been employed in countless works of art, such as *Venus Rising from the Sea* by Sandro Botticelli, *The Fifer* by Edouard Manet and the *David* by Michelangelo. As an alternative to the familiar frontal aspect of this pose, a rear view has been chosen to emphasize that the visual impression or impact of a subject is dependent more upon the spatial arrangement of its components than on the side that is presented to the viewer.

This principle is demonstrated in the illustration where the figure on the left is reduced to a silhouette that can be interpreted as either a frontal or rear view of the subject. The silhouette on the right shows the transformation of the neutral silhouette into a front view of the subject.

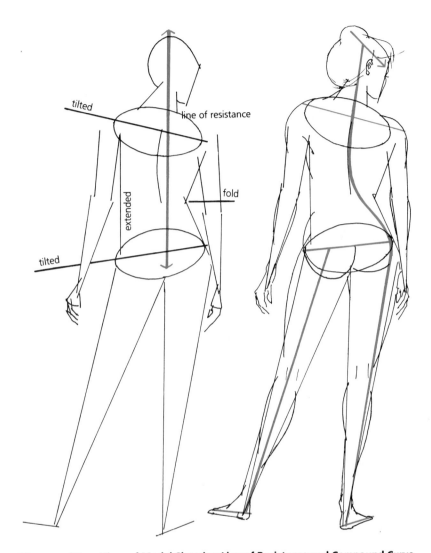

Diagram of Rear View of Model Showing Line of Resistance and Compound Curve

In the next diagram the subject is schematized. Both girdles, thoracic and pelvic, are tilted, causing an angle or fold on the right side of the body cavity (torso) and a thrusting line on the left side, indicating tension. The line of resistance indicates the medial aspect or inner planes of the right leg. (Shifting the weight from the right foot to the left would reverse the pattern; the line of resistance would indicate the inner plane of the left leg.) A helpful rule in gauging the *dynamics* of the human figure is that *the head is always located over the foot that is supporting most of the weight.* Drawing a line from the center of the head to the weight-bearing foot indicates the single line of resistance. The figure on the right has been *contoured* by applying a series of short and long arcs on opposite sides of the angular geometric triangles that symbolize the principal structural components of the figure. The spatial arrangement of the limbs, the thoracic and pelvic girdles, the spine and the head suggests a graceful compound curve *buttressed* by the angular thrust of the left leg.

The Foot and the Leg

The structure of the human limb is based upon the principle of the lever, as illustrated in the diagram. Placing a sheet of paper with its upper edge on the *base line* indicated in the diagram will show that, with the exception of their extremities, the leg, arm and to a great degree the thumb and fingers are fundamentally similar in both function and shape. The arm and leg are especially alike. This similarity in function and shape is shown in the diagram of the leg and arm.

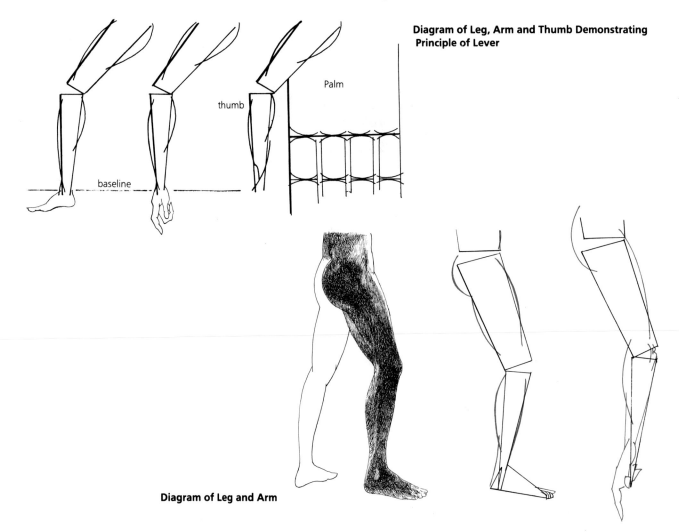

Diagram of Leg, Arm and Thumb Demonstrating Principle of Lever

Palm

thumb

baseline

Diagram of Leg and Arm

A vertical line indicates the line of resistance in the diagrams of the front view of the leg. The horizontal line represents the earth. A short, angled thrust near the base of the line of resistance indicates the foot (*a*). The addition of another line, angled toward the center of gravity, the line of resistance, suggests the basic scheme of the limb (*b*). The addition of opposing arcs (*c*) symbolizing muscular mass begins to establish the front view of the human leg. Placing a compressed arc at the base of the triangle projects the foot forward and lends it volume (*d*).

The next illustration demonstrates the rotation of the leg from side view to back view. The vertical line of resistance remains the same. However, lengthening the angle at its base (*a*) indicates the longitudinal arch of the foot viewed from the side. The leg is rotated from a side view to a rear view by the addition of minor detail (*b, c, d, e,*). Notice that the triangle representing the structural scheme of the human limb remains essentially the same regardless of the viewpoint.

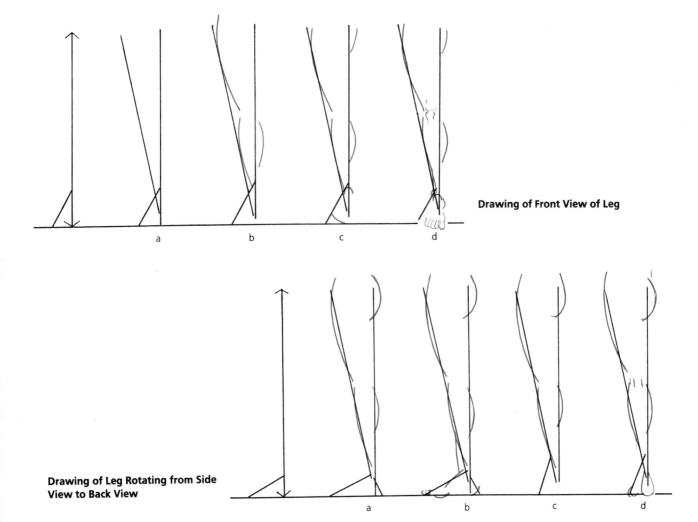

Drawing of Front View of Leg

a   b   c   d

Drawing of Leg Rotating from Side View to Back View

a   b   c   d

In the standing figure the model has assumed a position that demonstrates how the line of resistance, which indicates the center of gravity, can be used as a reference in drawing the figure in a standing pose. The line of resistance follows the inner plane of the leg that is supporting most of the weight, in this case the left. The edge or outer plane of the left leg angles inward toward the line of resistance in diagram *a*. Diagram *b* illustrates how the lower section of the human figure can be simply stated with several thrusting lines and arcs. See the drawing by Egon Schiele (last illustration in Chapter 6) in which he effectively adopted the scheme shown in *b*.

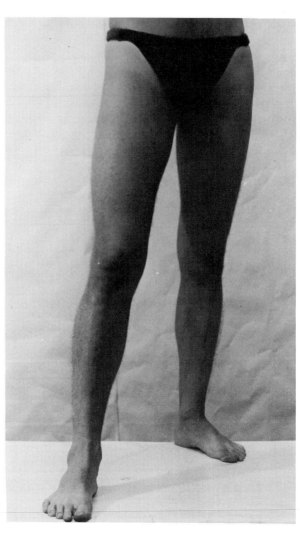

Photo and Diagrams of Lower Half of Standing Figure Showing Line of Resistance

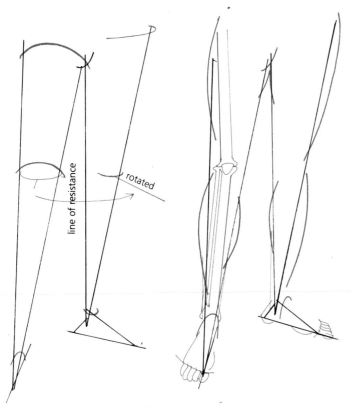

line of resistance

rotated

a   b

EXERCISE

Refer to the photograph of the side and rear views of legs as you copy the diagrams of the side and back of the foot, beginning with the basic triangular symbols. Then complete the contours with a series of short and long arcs.

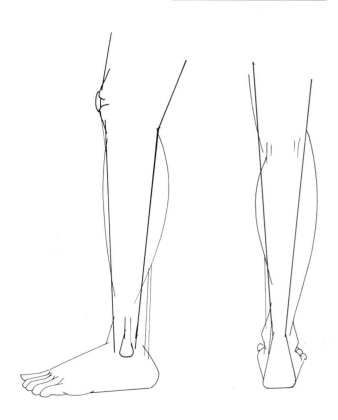

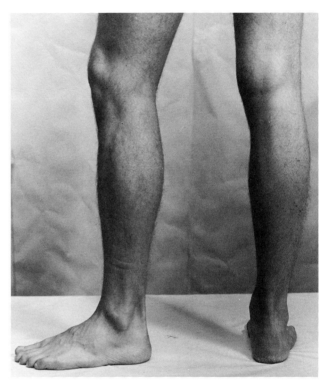

Photo and Diagram of Side and Rear Views of Legs

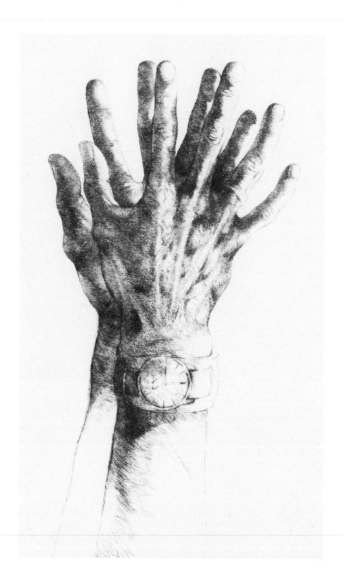

Adrian van Suchtelen, *Hands,* **dry point, 9" x 7¹/₂" (23 x 19 cm)**

The Arm and the Hand

The arm from the shoulder to the finger tips may be perceived as a unit composed of three segments, the upper arm, forearm and hand. In the schematic diagram, the principle points to look for when analyzing the arm are:

1. The gradual reduction of muscular mass represented by the circles as they proceed from the shoulder to the wrist.

2. The digital triangle which defines the plane that serves as a base for the thumb and borders the transverse arch.

3. The transverse arch located in the middle of the hand, offering clues to the action and position of the hand.

The appearance of the arm changes when the hand is rotated. Refer to the illustration showing both the back and the palm of the hand. By quickly shifting your view from *a* to *b,* you will see that the rotation involves the whole arm. Notice the outward angle of the forearm in *b,* and how it expands at the joint of the elbow.

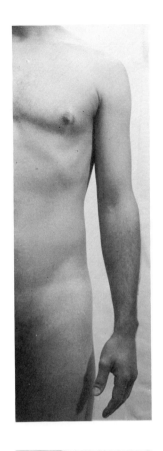

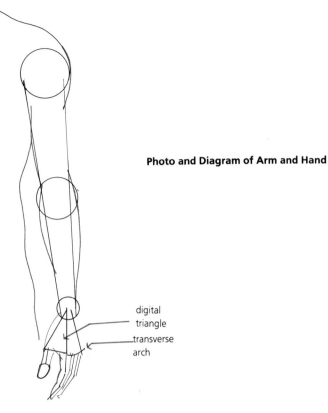

Photo and Diagram of Arm and Hand

digital
triangle

transverse
arch

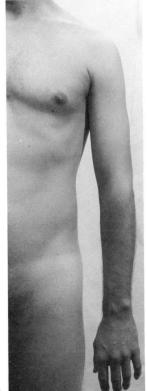

a

Arm and Back of Hand

transverse
arch

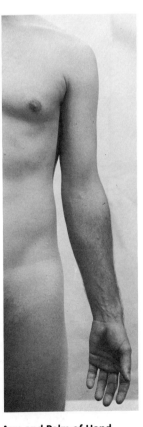

b

Arm and Palm of Hand

arm expands
at elbow joint

transverse
arch

arcs project
fingers

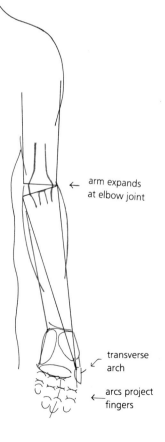

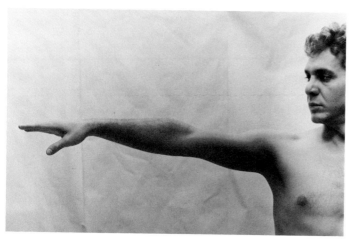

The diagrams of the extended arm and the foreshortened arm are shown to progress from the shoulder through the hand in three phases: upper arm, forearm and hands. *The hand is the final phase of the arm.* In *a* the circles represent the beginning of each phase at the shoulder, the elbow and the wrist. The decreasing muscular mass of the arm is demonstrated by the decreasing size of the circles. In *b* the extended arm is compressed on the picture plane and the circles are accordingly indicated closer together with the addition of opposing arcs. The arm is foreshortened without depending on an *outline*. The digital triangle is also compressed in accordance with the foreshortened hand.

Photo and Diagram of Extended Right Arm

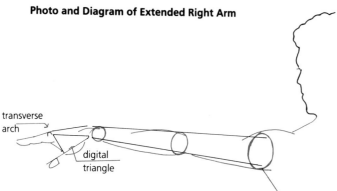

transverse arch

digital triangle

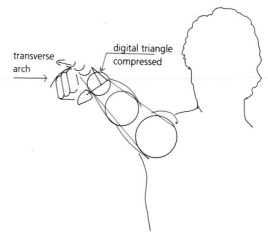

transverse arch

digital triangle compressed

Photo and Diagram of Foreshortened Right Arm

 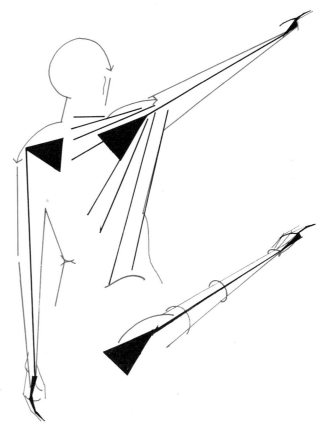

Photo and Diagram of Source and Extent of Right Arm

The model in the photograph has assumed a pose that demonstrates the source and extent of the arm. When the arm is raised the entire upper half of the muscular–skeletal system is activated. *The arm does not begin at the shoulder,* as shown in the diagram of the dorsal base of the arm. The arm rises from the pelvis and lateral side of the spinal column like an open half of a cone, activates the scapula, then continues as the solid half of the cone toward its apex in one finger of the hand. The complete action can be simplified by a modified triangle with the spinal column as its base. A front view of the upper half of the figure would be similar. Notice the tilt of the scapulas and how they conform to the action. One-half of the upper body is active, the other is passive. In the diagram showing the arm from the shoulder, the semicircles not only indicate how the arm is foreshortened, but also separate the solid section of the *cone,* scapula to wrist, from the open section, spine and pelvis to scapula.

Foreshortening

Foreshortening, like perspective, is a valuable and reliable graphic device in visual art that is not easily mastered. This is especially noticeable when the subject is the human figure. An exercise that has proven helpful is based upon working from a model whose limbs are arranged in both extended and flexed positions.

EXERCISE

Work from the photograph of the model with upraised arm or a live model in the same pose. Develop a schematic drawing in which the volumes, planes, spatial locations and positions of the subject's limbs are featured. The result will likely resemble details of the study for a large painting by Luca Cambiasco (*Martyrdom of Saint Lawrence,* Chapter 6).

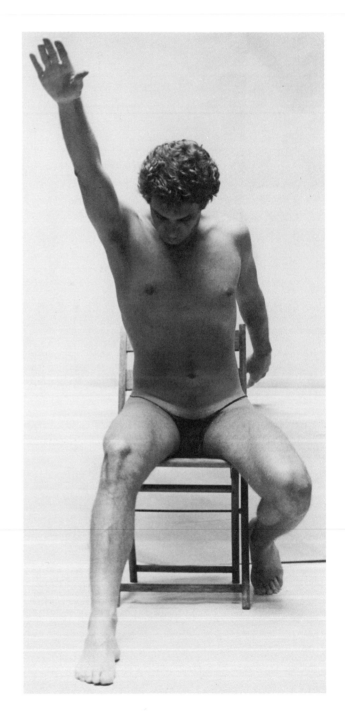

Seated Model with Upraised Arm

A solution to the problem of foreshortening the limbs of the subject is demonstrated in the diagrams of foreshortening. The model has assumed a pose in which the limbs are extended both toward and away from the viewer, above and below eye level. In *a* the torso, head and limbs are indicated proportionately in relation to the amount of two-dimensional space each occupies on the picture plane. The amount of space required depends upon whether the limbs are extended or flexed and upon the angle from which they are viewed. The introduction of semicircular arcs at the source of the left thigh and uplifted right arm not only locate the top plane of the left thigh and the lower plane of the right arm, but also place them, respectively, below eye level and above eye level. A tracing or copy of *b* will reveal the effectiveness of the *arc* and the *angle* as a visual device. Alternating or reversing the convex or concave aspect of the arcs immediately changes the movement or position of a projection. Examples are shown in the elbow of the left arm and the ankle of the left leg.

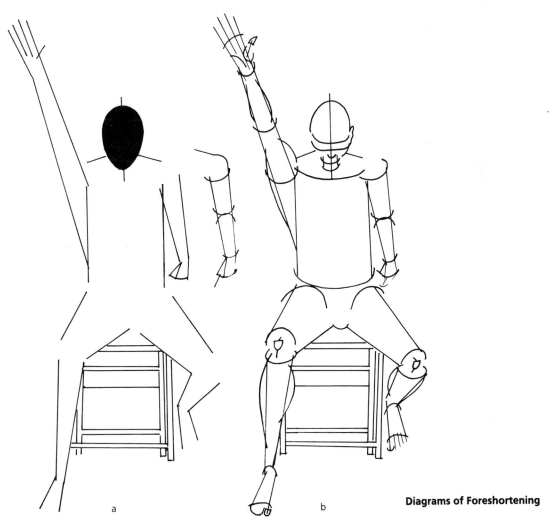

a   b   **Diagrams of Foreshortening**

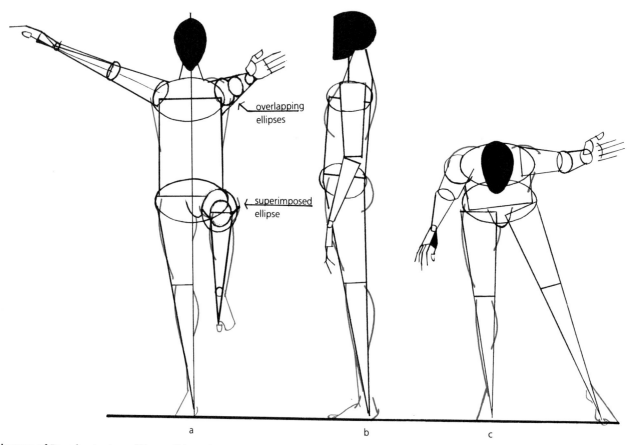

overlapping
ellipses

superimposed
ellipse

a

b

c

Diagram of Foreshortening of Front, Side and Torso of Figure

In part *a* of the diagram of front, side and torso foreshortening, the extended right arm and leg of the figure are depicted by elongated triangles, while the foreshortened left arm and thigh are represented by shortened or compressed triangles. The decreasing masses of the shoulder, elbow and wrist of the extended right arm are indicated in cross section by a series of ellipses diminishing in size as they progress from the shoulder to the wrist. The left arm is foreshortened by overlapping circles representing the shoulder, elbow and wrist within the *compressed* triangle, while the left thigh is projected forward by overlapping two circles within an extremely compressed triangle. The larger circle indicates the thigh as it emerges from the pelvis, and the smaller circle represents its terminus at the knee, and the lower condyle of the femur. In *b* the ellipses representing the thoracic and pelvic girdles, and the rectangle indicating the torso have been constricted to present the standing figure in profile. In *c* the upper section of the figure has been foreshortened by superimposing the thoracic girdle over the pelvic girdle, while the arms are shown in varied positions by overlapping the ellipses symbolizing the joints within modified triangles.

The sequence through which the foreshortened limbs may be conceived and drawn is demonstrated in the diagram of the foreshortening of the left leg.

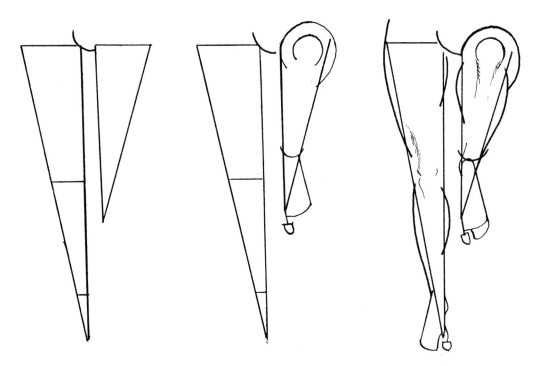

Diagram of Foreshortening of Left Leg

Gene Hackman, *Hands,* **dry point, 6¹/₂" x 9"
(16.5 x 23 cm)**

The Hand

The anxiety experienced by the beginner confronted with the challenging problem of drawing the human hand may be avoided by an introduction to several of its structural features. This usually requires a revision in how you conceive one of the most efficient, precisely organized structures in existence. Contrary to what it seems to be, an assembly of digits emerging from the wrist, the hand is the final segment, or phase, of the arm. Often, even the most subtle of its movements involves the majority of the muscles of the forearm and, in many instances, those of the upper arm and torso. Familiarizing yourself with the key factors of the hand will simplify the process of appraising and depicting its schematic pattern. The following exercise is designed to help you locate, identify and eventually utilize key factors that govern the function and shape of the human hand.

EXERCISE

While referring to either the photograph of the right hand, your own or a model's hand, copy or trace the diagram of the hand. During the process you should become aware of the following factors:

1. The hand, when extended, is almost as long as the forearm.

2. The fingers are fundamentally angular. A cross section of each would be rectangular in shape. Each finger may be conceived as an elongated jointed cube.

3. Careful consideration should be given to the triangular interstices that separate the fingers along the transverse arch.

4. The strategic location of the digital triangle, placed at a right angle to the transverse arch, allows the thumb directly to oppose each finger.

5. A logical appraisal of the hand suggests that it could very well be conceived as a *four-fingered* structure with the thumb as a separate pivotal device essential for the proper functioning of the arm as well as the hand.

6. The thumb, beginning from its solid anchorage at the base of the digital triangle, has a specialized shape that thrusts outward with a short shaft that suddenly expands into a pressure-resisting wedgelike tip.

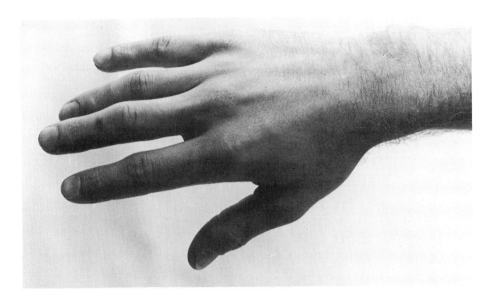

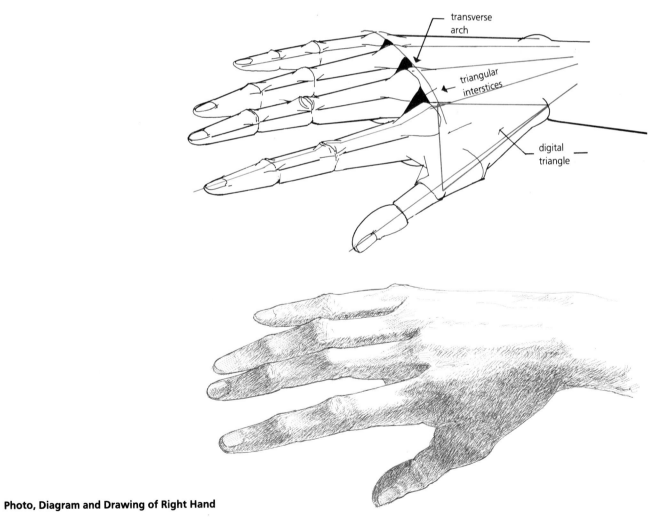

transverse
arch

triangular
interstices

digital
triangle

Photo, Diagram and Drawing of Right Hand

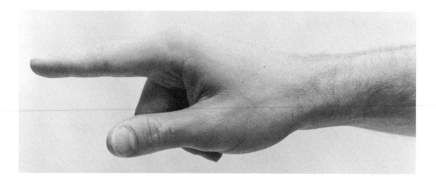

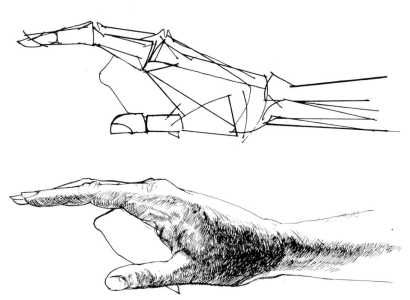

**Photo, Diagram and Drawing of Thumb and
Index Finger in Profile**

The tonal pattern of the drawing of the hand is based upon the planes and contours resulting from the key structural factors shown in the schematic diagram. The diagram based on the photograph of the thumb and index finger in profile stresses the angular character of the hand. Emphasis is placed on the sharply delineated ridges, contours and planes that result from the internal meshing of joints, balanced levers and cablelike tendons and muscles of the hand. The structural features are schematized with a series of overlapping and juxtaposed triangles and rectangles, that is, the plane of the digital triangle, the base, shaft and tip of the thumb, the condyles of the ulna and radius that constitute part of the wrist, and the side planes of the index and middle finger. The contours and tonal pattern of the drawing are based upon the features in the diagram.

The photograph of the open palm of the hand shows its fundamental makeup. The palm is designed to resist friction and pressure, which contrasts severely with the concisely engineered carpals and metacarpals it protects. The pattern of the palm consists of a circular array of padlike mounds surrounding a central depression. The exception is the thumb, which is indicated with a modified triangle, a rectangle and an outline of its tip.

Below the photograph are student examples, one showing the study in progress and the other completed. The approach in each study is based upon extended form drawing (Chapter 5), in which any section or element of a subject is completed with a single motion, an act comparable to inscribing a closed letter of the alphabet (for example o or a). The segments of the palm were completed with a series of ovals and rectangles, each inscribed with a single looping motion. The segmented pads of the fingers are described with short opposing arcs adjacent to each other.

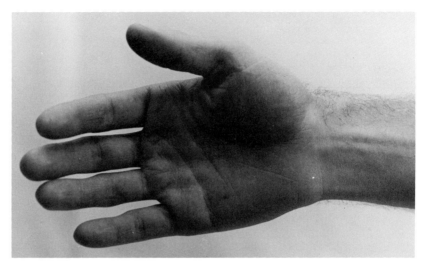

Photo of Open Palm of Hand

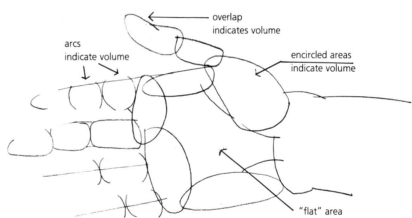

arcs
indicate volume

overlap
indicates volume

encircled areas
indicate volume

"flat" area

Student Study of Palm of Hand in Progress

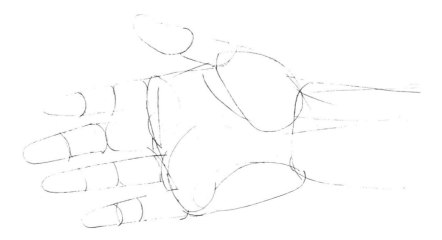

Student Study of Palm of Hand Completed

Kathe Kollwitz, *Self Portrait,* lithograph, National Gallery of Art, Washington, Rosenwald Collection

The Head

The vertebrate head, in contrast to the limbs that are designed for spatial extension, is planned for space-saving compactness. It is structured to enclose space with an elaborate, precisely proportioned arrangement of arches, domes, buttresses and vaults. Variations in the vertebrate head seem infinite, yet the fundamental elements present in all heads—amphibian, reptilian, mammalian and so on—are based on common structural elements that can be detected and simplified through schematic drawing.

In comparative anatomy the heads of most quadrupeds have been compared to a three-room, one-story house extending horizontally from the spinal column. The first room contains the central nervous system, the middle contains the sensory systems and the front room, the jaws. The human head has been compared to a three-room, three-story house vertically stacked. The lower room contains the jaws, the second floor contains the sensory systems and the upper floor, the central nervous system.

The fundamental structure and shape of the human head is determined by *four arches* located at each *level,* and their relationship to the cranium. They are shown in the diagram of the human skull as: 1) the frontal arch (frontal bone), upper level; 2) the zygomatic arch (zygomatic and malar bone combined), middle level; 3) the maxillar arch (maxilla, upper jaw) and 4) the mandibular arch (mandible, lower jaw), lower level.

An important visual device for conceiving and depicting the head is the imaginary *medial line* of the facial plane. It serves two purposes. First, it emphasizes the symmetrical structure of the head. Second, it is a key for gauging and determining the position of the head in space. In the frontal view of the head this line extends through the middle of the facial plane from the top of the frontal bone to the mandible. In the side view of the head it is situated at right angles to the zygomatic arch and extends upward to the edge of the frontal arch and downward toward a point slightly behind the frontal aspect of the mandibular arch (the chin).

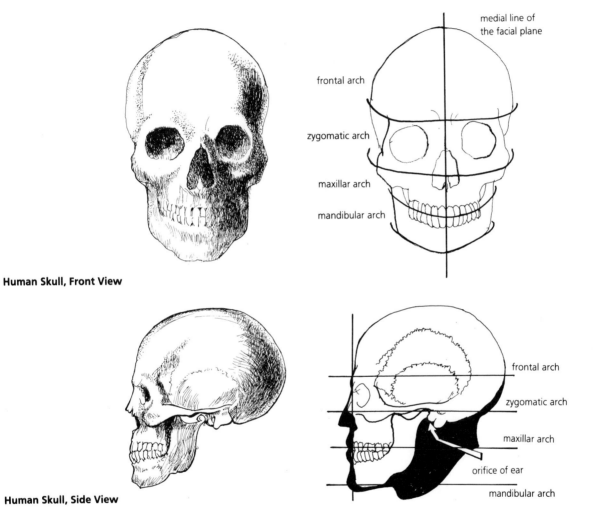

Human Skull, Front View

Human Skull, Side View

A recommended procedure for either analyzing or drawing the head, regardless of its position in space, is by properly gauging the angle of the zygomatic arch as it intersects the *medial line* at the middle of the head. At eye level the arch crosses the line at a right angle. At either higher or lower levels, the angle increases. This relationship follows the principles regarding optics and perception that are covered in the section dealing with the arc and the angle in Chapter 6.

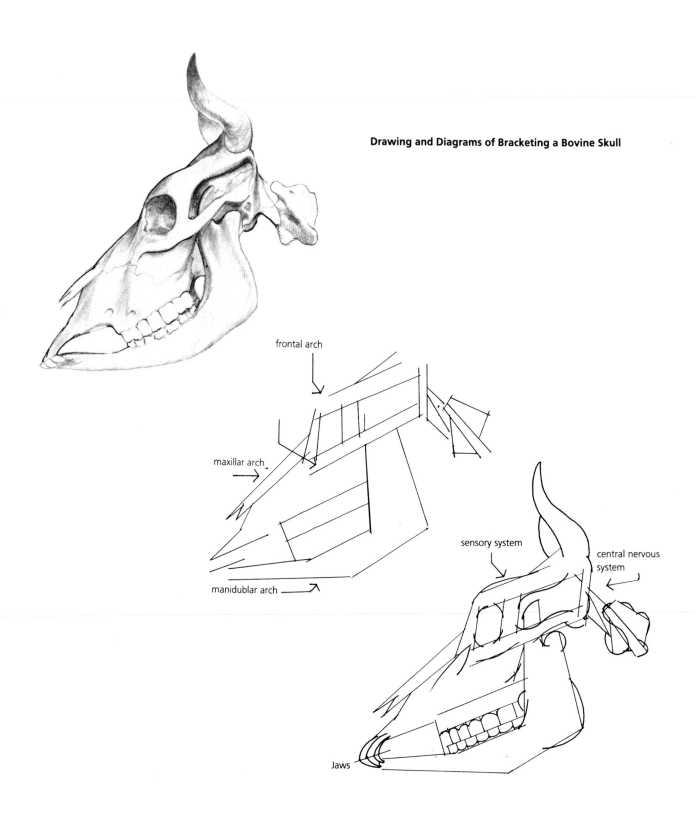

Drawing and Diagrams of Bracketing a Bovine Skull

frontal arch

maxillar arch

manidublar arch

sensory system

central nervous system

Jaws

Bracketing

A simple, effective approach toward conceiving the principal structural features of the vertebrate head is generally known as *bracketing*. This method is illustrated for a bovine skull. The contours, curvatures, hollows and projections of the skull are contained within a *grid* of straight, mostly parallel lines and finalized with a few curvilinear accents.

Bracketing is a direct method for appraising a subject in which the amount of space it contains or activates is comparable to the substance that surrounds it. It is a process through which space and solidity are equally considered and simultaneously indicated on the picture plane (The Grid System, Chapter 6). Neither space nor solidity is awarded priority. An example is the illustration in which the spatial as well as the solid constituents of a concrete block are simultaneously indicated with a grid of intersecting vertical and horizontal lines. The accompanying diagram of the skull is also bracketed to indicate the structural features most responsible for the shape of the human head. The sockets of the eyes are suggested by two horizontal lines representing the lower edge of the frontal arch and the upper ridge of the zygomatic arch. The short vertical thrusts intersecting the horizontal lines indicate the rims of the sockets and the temporal bones. The nasal region is plotted with the tip of a triangle with a base that encompasses the semicylindrical maxillar and mandibular arches. The pattern is comparable to the bracket indicating both the solid and spatial elements of the concrete block.

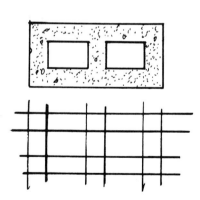

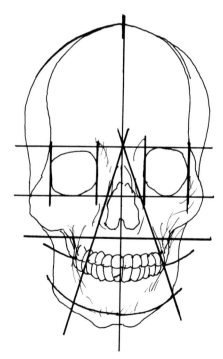

Diagram of the Bracketing of a Concrete Block and the Human Head, Front View

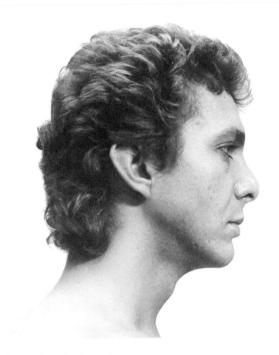

Photo of Model in Profile

At first the profile of the human head seems to be enclosed within a meandering, undulating outline. An objective analysis reveals that the profile results from the *forward* thrust of the four arches of the skull—the frontal bone, the zygomatic arch, the maxilla, the mandible—as they project in varying degrees *beyond* the medial line of the facial plane.

A reliable approach toward analyzing and depicting the human head in profile is illustrated in three stages in which the particular or individual characteristics of the model are ignored:

a. The neck and cranium are represented by a looping arc on a stem, in this pose resembling a question mark in reverse. The facial plane is stated with a vertical line. The four arches are symbolized with four horizontal lines.

b. The four arcs representing the arches of the skull are extended proportionally beyond the medial line. So is the nasal structure. At this stage the lower arcs representing the maxilla and mandible are joined together with a short arc that indicates the pronounced convex assemblage of the teeth.

c. The muscular systems of the mouth and lips are added to the convex arc as the profile is finalized with a linear contour.

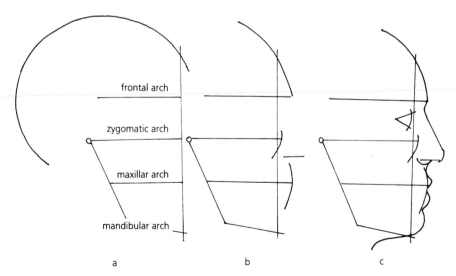

frontal arch

zygomatic arch

maxillar arch

mandibular arch

a

b

c

Three Stages of Depicting the Human Head in Profile

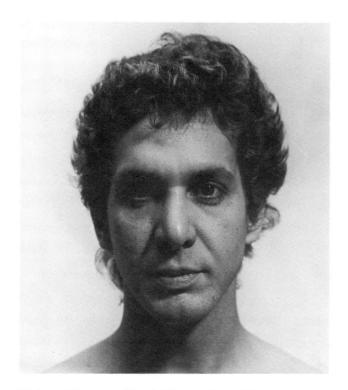

Photo and Diagram of Head at Eye Level, Front View

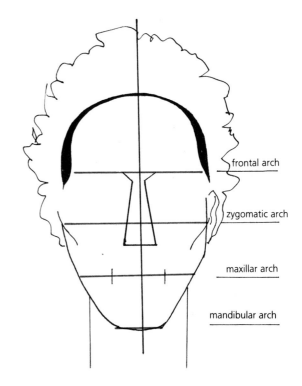

frontal arch

zygomatic arch

maxillar arch

mandibular arch

The frontal view of the head is illustrated at eye level. The head is bracketed with four parallel horizontal lines that intersect the medial line of the facial plane.

Beverly Worlock, *Head Study,* **charcoal pencil, 8" x 10" (20.5 x 25.5 cm), with diagram**

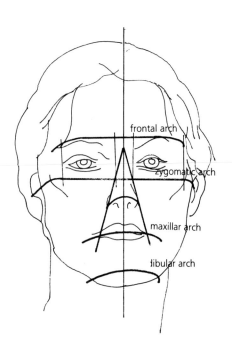

The drawing of the head viewed from slightly below eye level and a bit to the right was conceived with a grid in which the prongs of the arches are angled downward to indicate the planes of the side of the head above eye level. The lower arches of the maxilla and mandible that appeared as straight horizontal lines in the eye-level diagram have been curved to show the semicylindrically shaped rims of the jaws seen from below.

The head tilted back has been bracketed by superimposing the arches of the skull within a narrow area of the picture plane. Viewed in this position the variations in the size and contour of each arch are clearly distinguishable: the rounded edge of the frontal bone that forms the upper ridge of each eye socket, the angular zygomatic arch that forms the lower ridge of the eye sockets and establishes the widest section of the head, and the compact semicylindrical maxillar and mandibular arches that together form the jaws and mouth. The bottom of the nose is indicated by the short *compressed* arc emerging from the middle of the zygomatic arch.

The forward tilt or bowed position is depicted by reversing the position of the arches and overlapping them within one-third of the area occupied by the whole image. The cranium is extended over two-thirds of the area designated for the image.

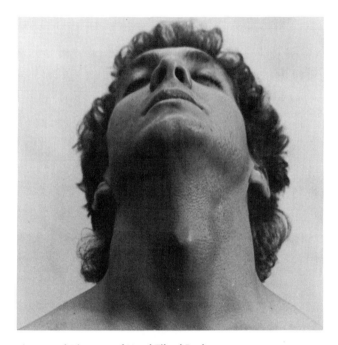

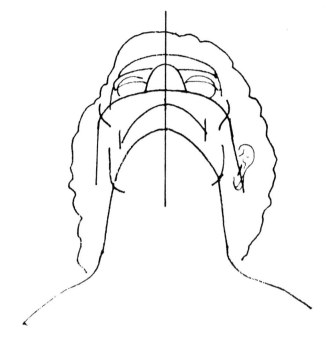

Photo and Diagram of Head Tilted Back

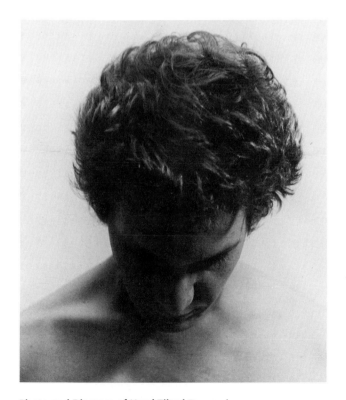

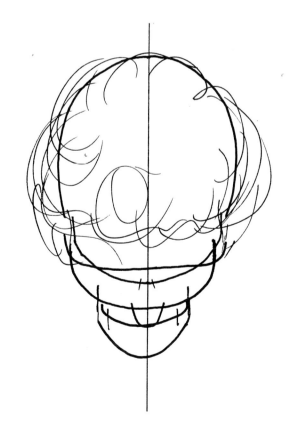

Photo and Diagram of Head Tilted Forward

Richard Feynman, *Head Study*, charcoal pencil, with diagrams

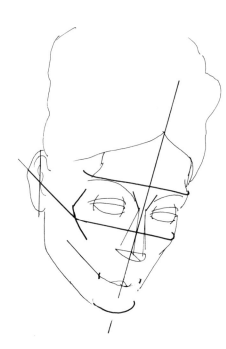

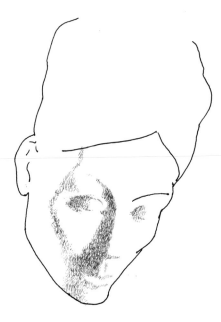

The facial plane and right side of the head tilted gently forward, viewed at eye level, is shown completed and in a bracket version. The frontal plane has been placed in position by *rotating* the medial line clockwise and intersecting it at right angles with the four arches of the head. The side of the head is indicated by turning the ends or *prongs* of the arches upward. Notice how the line of the arc representing the zygomatic arch bisects the orifice of the ear. The second diagram shows the initial phase of applying tone to the bracketed linear concept. Tone is applied to the leading edge of the arches as they turn sharply to separate the facial plane from the side of the head.

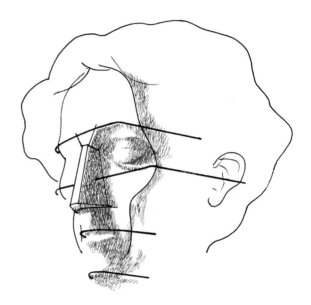

Alfonse Legros, *Head of a Man,* **silverpoint, The Metropolitan Museum of Art, New York, Gift of the Artist**

The silverpoint drawing by Alfonse Legros conveys more than an accurate likeness of an individual. The image is imbued with a sense of loftiness and dignity that is mainly due to the locations and angles of the four arches of the skull. The subject was lifted above eye level by sharply angling the arcs downward as they traverse and define the boundary separating the facial and side planes of the head. The accompanying diagram demonstrates how the *cross-hatch* technique was first applied to insure the development of a tonal pattern consistent with structural elements (anatomy) of the facial and side planes of the head.

The mixed media drawing by Terry Stout placed at eye level was conceived through imagination. The arches of the head, particularly the frontal and zygomatic arches, have been freely modified and rearranged to conform to the projected image. The artist made the following comments about the drawing:

In this series of drawings I was at once trying to convey the importance of a single human being, and inherent isolation. The basic shapes (the oval of the head and the irregular rectangle of the torso) are contained shapes, keeping the visual activity within the forms and not interacting with space around them, therefore isolation. The figure is placed centrally to further enhance the quietness of the image.

Terry Stout, *Human Being, Babylon Series,* **mixed media 30" x 22" (76 x 56 cm)**

Beverly Worlock has drawn a three-quarter view of a slightly tilted head above eye level. The proper angle was gauged by slanting the arches of the skull downward and to the left of an imaginary line, extending from the zygomatic arch to the chin, that separates the facial plane from the side of the head. The left side of the head is further emphasized by placing the ear downward and to the right of the same dividing line.

In the drawing of a head in profile the same artist found it necessary to compress the frontal aspect of the arches of the skull and its facial features into a narrow area of the picture plane. With the head in a level position, as shown, the zygomatic arch extends horizontally from a point slightly above the base of the occipital bone (base of the skull) through the orifice of the ear to the middle of the nose, thus indicating the middle of the head.

Beverly Worlock, *Miriam,* pen and ink wash, 8" x 10" (20.5 x 25.5 cm)

Beverly Worlock, *Bob,* pen and ink, 10" x 14" (25.5 x 35.5 cm)

Billy Royse, *Head of a Clown,* **pencil and pastel, 16" x 24" (40.5 x 61 cm)**

Dimitrius Vilan, *Head of a Clown,* **charcoal, 12" x 18" (30.5 x 46 cm)**

Billy Royse's *Head of a Clown* is a parody on the subject of clowns. The hidden internal structure of the head has been reorganized into a cubistic montage. It is one of many examples of a general obsession with the subject as well as the image of the clown. Dimitrius Vilan's drawing is also called *Head of a Clown,* but the title is incidental. It is a competent graphic version of the individual characteristics (likeness) perceived by the human eye, in this case, a side view of a middle-aged individual posing with the headpiece of a clown. Both versions, regardless of imagery or intent, are based upon an understanding of the structural elements of the head.

Lorraine Grandier Walter, *Kareen Walter Scott,*
oil, with diagram

The content of a work of art often exhibits qualities beyond those suggested by the title. The merits of a portrait should not depend upon whether or not an authentic likeness of the subject has been achieved. Lorraine Grandier Walter's portrait is not only an accurate likeness of her daughter, but is a subtle yet convincing impression of youthful, graceful feminity. She used the *wet to wet* method in oil painting, a technique that requires skillful handling of the medium as well as accurate perception. The tonal values in its design have been restricted to a narrow range or *key* within the upper level of the tonal scale. The lowest tone is slightly above a middle tone, the highest is white. The oval character of the head has been emphasized by the curvilinear descent of the hair as it sweeps past the contours of the facial plane to encounter and engage the *squarish* shape and the vertical folds of the blouse.

Pencil Drawing From a Drapery Study by Leonardo da Vinci

Drapery

Drapery, whether featured in the twists and folds of a worker's garment in a lithograph by Diego Rivera, in the flowing sculptured toga of a Roman emperor, as a backdrop for a nude by Edgar Degas or in a still life by Paul Cezanne, remains one of the most important components of expressive design. At rest or in a neutral state, drapery, like water, may be considered an inert substance capable of being activated by circumstance and environment through the force of gravity. Like a wave hitting a rock, drapery assumes predictable dynamic patterns.

A practical way of reading the folds in drapery is to reduce their contours, convolutions, tension and spirals to four basic types: *gravity folds, tension folds, contour folds* and *reaction folds.* Like all basic or elementary components, the various types combine to form the infinite, composite variations in drapery fold patterns that have proven to be a major influence on the content or subject matter of representational art.

The basic anatomy of drapery may be easily demonstrated. A length of cloth, a shirt or a jacket suspended from a single support such as a nail or peg will immediately assume a definite pattern, showing the folds radiating from the point of support. An analogy would be the ripples and foam radiating from an obstruction like a stone or a stick in a swiftly flowing stream of water. Folds descending from either a pointed support or an extended support—an arm, thigh, rod, belt—are referred to as *gravity folds.* Gravity folds are illustrated in the photo and diagram showing a single support.

Folds from drapery extended between two supporting points, also illustrated, are referred to as *tension folds.* Either a gradual or sudden release of gravitational tension as a fold comes to rest or encounters an obstacle is referred to as a *reaction fold.* An action comparable to a wave striking a rock, folds in drapery superimposed or draped over an extended projection like a shoulder, thigh, arm or head of the human figure, are referred to as *contour folds.*

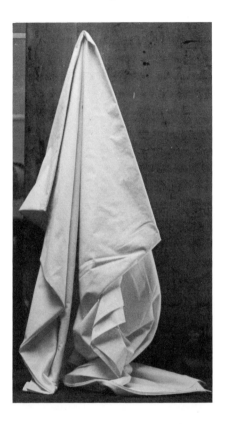

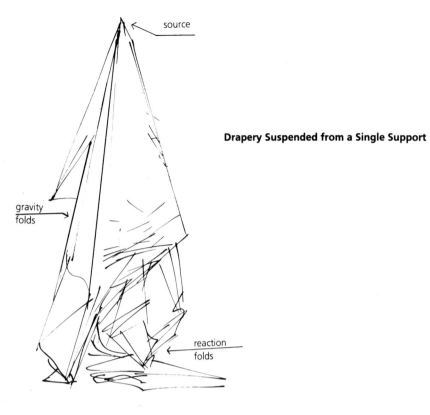

Drapery Suspended from a Single Support

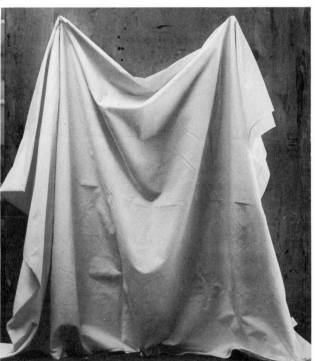

Drapery Suspended from Two Supporting Points

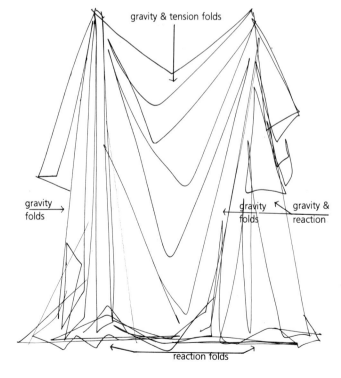

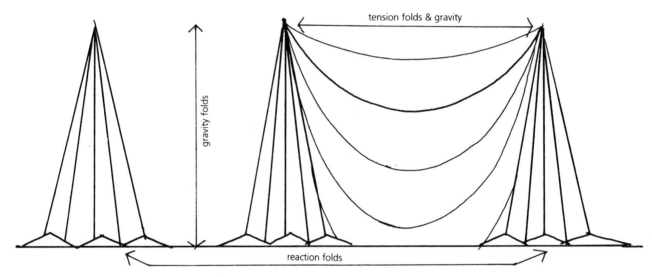

Gravity, Reaction and Tension Folds Schematically Diagramed

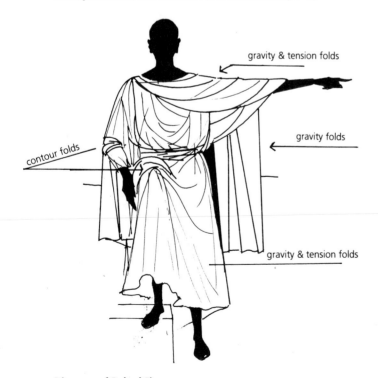

Diagram of Robed Figure

Gravity folds and reaction folds are shown schematized, suspended from a single point of support. Gravity folds and tension folds suspended between two points of support are also shown schematized. The tension folds in this illustration are not tightly stretched, resulting in a series of descending loops in which the characteristics of the gravity fold and the tension fold are combined. In each diagram the lower edges of the drapery, resting on a horizontal plane, have been schematically indicated as reaction folds.

The standard or prototype robed figure prevalent in classical plastic and visual art is diagramed to illustrate how secondary folds are derived from the varied combinations of the primary folds: gravity, tension, contour and reaction.

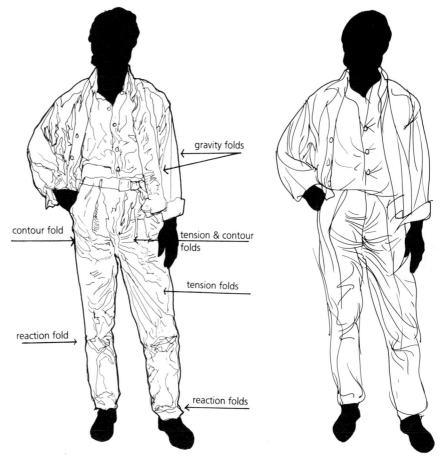

Photo and Diagrams of Clothed Figure

gravity folds

contour fold

tension & contour folds

tension folds

reaction fold

reaction folds

At first glance, a tracing of the photograph of the clothed figure reveals what seems to be a chaotic maze of creases and folds without order. Nevertheless, an *edited* version exposes rhythmic patterns that may be adopted as a linear interpretation of the subject. For example, the folds originating over the right thigh have been integrated with those of the left in developing a curvilinear flow of lines that, in descending, seem to perform a brief swirling dance at the knee before indicating a concluding gesture at the bottom of the garment.

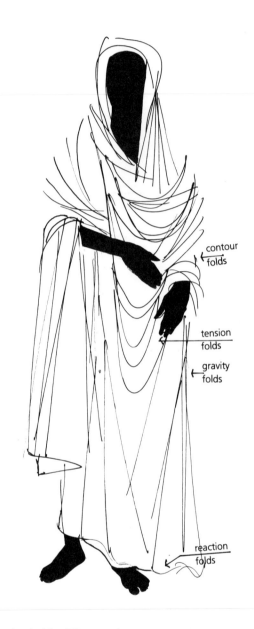

contour
folds

tension
folds

gravity
folds

reaction
folds

Photo and Diagram of Standing Draped Figure

The unmistakable difference between the fold systems of a fully draped, standing figure and a fully draped, seated figure should be carefully noted. Normally, in a standing draped figure, represented in the photograph, the fold system is dominated by *vertical* or nearly vertical gravity folds. In the diagram the vertical flow of the gravity folds is balanced schematically by a countermotion contributed by tension folds extending from shoulder to shoulder and looping downward between the contour folds rounding out the upper right arm and left forearm of the figure.

Photo of Seated Draped Figure

Contour Drawing of Seated Draped Figure

In contrast, the fold system of the seated draped figure represented in the photograph is dominated by tension, contour and reaction folds. The gravity folds have been compressed. The contour drawing is based upon recognizing and utilizing the key or main folds of the fully draped figure in a seated position represented in the photograph. An *action* sketch of the same pose stresses the angular dynamics of the fold systems when drapery is compressed.

Action Sketch of Seated Draped Figure

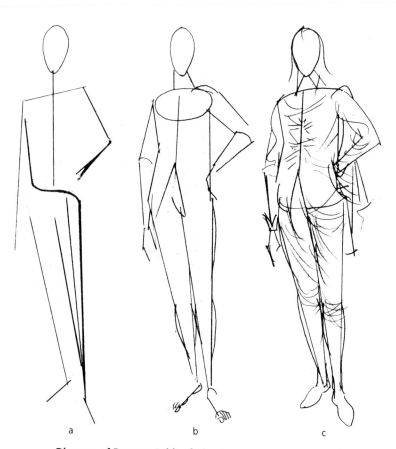

Diagram of Drapery Folds of *Blue Boy*

Thomas Gainsborough, *Blue Boy*, oil, Henry E. Huntington Library and Art Gallery, Pasadena

An extraordinary combination of a hidden compound curve balanced with the dynamics of fold patterns is the basis for the concept and design of *Blue Boy* by Thomas Gainsborough. The compound curve is the result of the spatial adjustment of the main structural elements of the human body to the force of gravity.

The drapery folds of *Blue Boy* are diagramed in the illustration. The curve in *a* is shown descending from the right shoulder to sweep around the hips and terminate in the toe of the left foot. The curve is emphasized in *b* by tilting the pelvic girdle and adding an obtuse angle to represent the extended side. At this point the contours of the tightly fitted garments are suggested with a minimum number of long and short arcs. The fold patterns in *c* have been skillfully administered to: 1) position the viewpoint halfway between the top and bottom of the subject, 2) lend volume to the limbs and 3) to harmonize with the spatial motion suggested by the hidden compound curve.

It is unfortunate that a skillfully rendered, sensitively conceived work should be marred by a weak interpretation of the right hand. Increasing the length of the forefinger and gently bending its tip toward the interior of the hat would oppose the rigidity of the thumb and complete the movement of the arm with a final graceful accent.

Charles White, ***General Moses,*** **dry brush and chinese ink,
Collection of Golden State Mutual, Afro-American Art**

The dynamic fold patterns of the drapery in the drawing by
Charles White serve several expressive and descriptive purposes. The contour folds are skillfully adjusted to emphasize the flexed and extended position of the arms, the
forward projection of the thighs and the volume of the
upper region of the figure. Also, as half circles (arcs), they
act as a counterpoint to the angular facets of the rock formations of the background. The gravity and tension folds
of the lower garment form an animated supporting base
for the triangular subject enclosed within a rectangular
environment.

Chapter 5

Extended

Form Drawing

All nature's structuring, associating and patterning must be based on triangles, because there is no structural validity otherwise. This is nature's basic structure and it is a model of life.

Richard Buckminster Fuller

EXTENDED FORM DRAWING may be considered the opposite of contained form drawing. In the latter approach form is reduced to a simple primary shape to be later defined by adding detail. In contrast, an *extended form drawing* is gradually developed by adding section after section to a basic preestablished nucleus. It is a formal method traditionally known as *overlapping*. When combined with schematic drawing, it becomes an effective tool for visualizing inorganic as well as organic form. It also helps to overcome a natural tendency to concentrate on the edges or outlines of form before analyzing and understanding the structural elements responsible for its appearance.

The extended form procedure is analogous to that of a sculptor working with clay as the medium and the human figure as the subject. The sculptor begins by placing a substantial chunk of clay on a supporting armature, roughly shaped to represent the pelvis. Next, the forms that constitute the human figure are extended upward, downward and laterally by deliberately adding masses of clay, section by section, to complete the spatial extensions of the limbs and the spinal thrust terminating in the head.

Extended form drawing has been applied to demonstrate the volume of a pear. In the middle diagram the volume has been indicated by two overlapping strokes of a pen, which are completed with a contour outline in the last diagram.

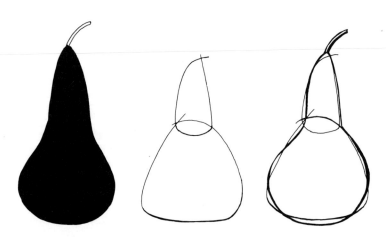

Albert Porter has indicated the principal structural elements
of a seated figure using this same approach. Notice the
overlapping geometric strokes that distinguish extended
form drawing.

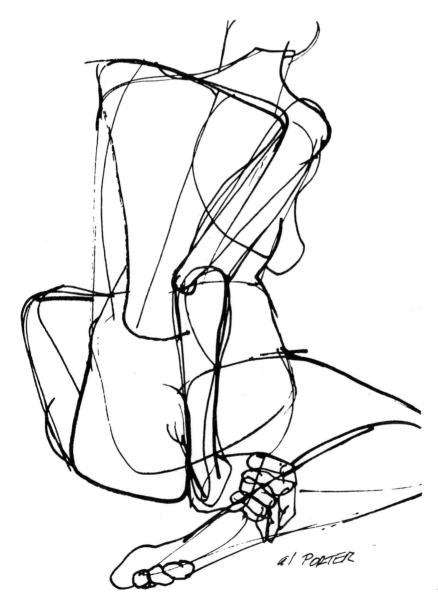

Albert Porter, *Seated Figure*, pen and ink

As a class experiment, students were asked to draw an outline of North America from a silhouetted version as shown in the illustration. A composite of the results revealed that most of the students became involved with the left and right sides of the image, and neglected its top, bottom and, most regretably, its *interior.* A large percentage of students overestimated the interior, the remainder underestimated it.

The problem was solved through extended form drawing, shown in three stages. First, the principal area of the shape is indicated with one encompassing stroke. Secondary projections are added by slightly superimposing them over the edges of the main area, as indicated in the middle diagram. Subsidiary projections are then added to form a basis for a final linear contour.

An analytical diagram of detail from Michelangelo's Sistine Chapel painting, *The Creation of Adam,* suggests that the hands of the Creator, as well as Adam's, could very well have been conceived through extended form drawing.

Silhouette of North America, with Overestimate and Underestimate

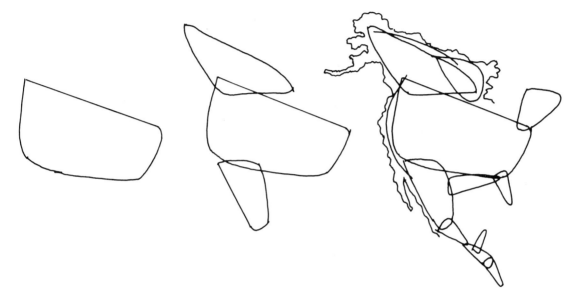

Extended Form Drawing of North America in Three Stages

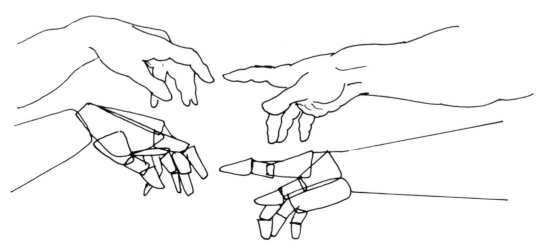

Diagram of Hands, Detail from Sistine Chapel Painting by Michelangelo

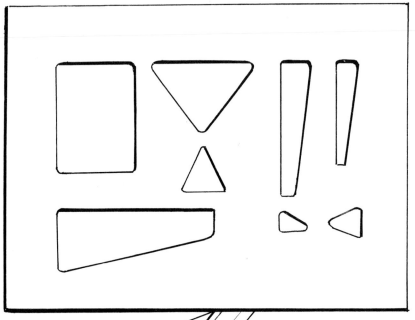

Template

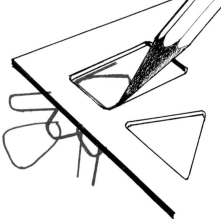

The deliberate, unhurried section-by-section procedure that distinguishes extended form drawing from other methods can be understood by experimenting with a template that may be cut out of cardboard or plastic. Transparent plastic is usually preferred. Follow the edges of the openings in the template with a soft pencil to simulate the tactile sensation essential to mastering the technique.

The importance of the sense of touch cannot be overemphasized. Each drawing concept, from schematic to contour drawing, relies in varying degrees upon movements and pressures that are monitored through touch. For example, in contour drawing the surface of the paper is contacted and sensed with cursive sweeping strokes of a pen, pencil or brush. In contrast, extended form drawing is realized by combining pressure with preconceived, deliberately inscribed geometric shapes.

The next illustration is an example of extended form drawing using the illustrated template. The result is a sharply defined hard-edged diagram of the structural elements of the human figure in an extended position. The photograph of the model in an extended pose (Chapter 4) was used as the basis for this drawing.

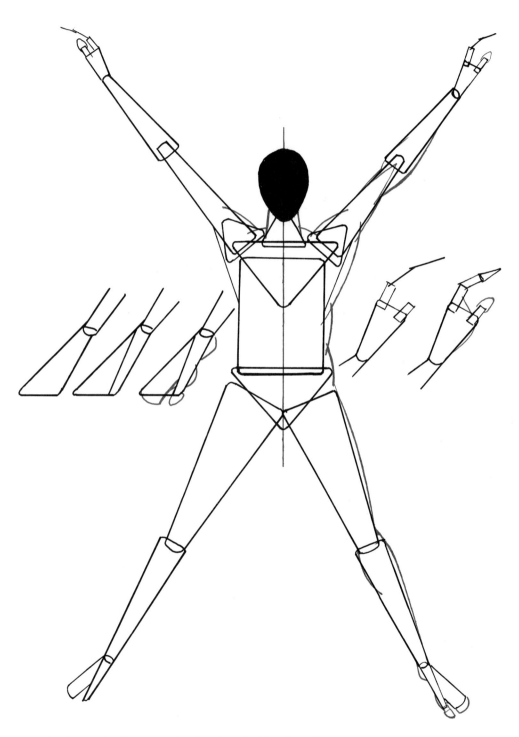

Example of Extended Form Drawing Developed with a Template

A study of the photograph of the female model is shown as it was developed in three stages. Beginning with the pelvic area the principal shapes that determine the appearance of the human figure are firmly stated. The muscular mass of the left shoulder and the gluteus are added in the middle diagram. The geometric shapes are contoured with a chisel-pointed carpenter's pencil, as shown in the final diagram.

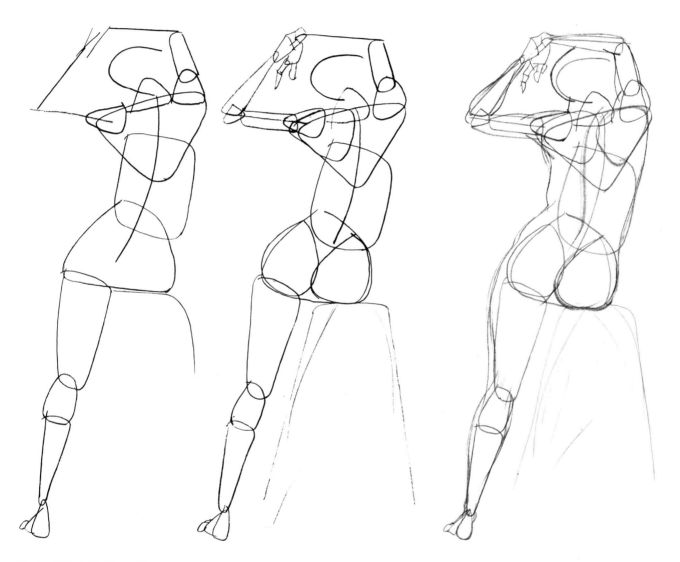

Study of Model in Three Stages

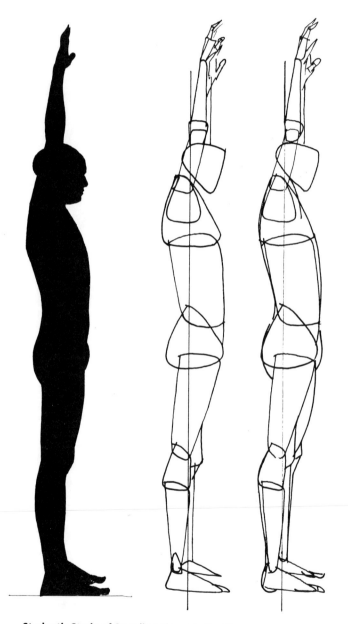

A student's example of the standing figure in profile demonstrates that the approach to the study is similar to the one used for the front and rear views of the human figure. The difference is in conceiving the torso, pelvic girdle and thoracic girdle, which, viewed from the side, are reduced in width. The study is shown in two stages after the model has been perceived as a silhouette (without detail). In the first stage the triangles and rectangles have been arranged to form a graceful compound curve based on the line of resistance, that is, with the torso tilted dorsally. A minimum amount of detail is added to complete a basis for a realistic, stylized or semiabstract image of the human figure.

EXERCISE

As an experiment, select a drawing and reduce it to its basic structural concept by applying the technique of extended form drawing. The illustration by David Schnabel and an analysis of it are based on extended form drawing.

Or, try depicting the same subject in different media. David Green has used charcoal and a modified extended form approach in his study for the ceramic piece, *Fledglings.* In both versions the design is based on dynamics, linear in the drawing and spatial in the ceramic. The upward rocketlike thrust manifested in the necks, heads and beaks of the subjects seems to emerge from an inert round base first conceived with overlapping shapes in the drawing—then with extended masses of clay in the ceramic.

Student's Study of Standing Figure in Profile

David Green, *Fledglings,* **ceramic, 14" (35.5 cm)**

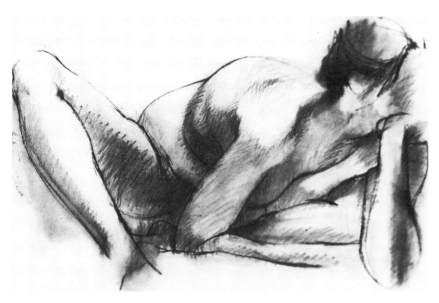

David Schnabel, *Study,* **NuPastel, 23" x 36" (58.5 x 91.5)**

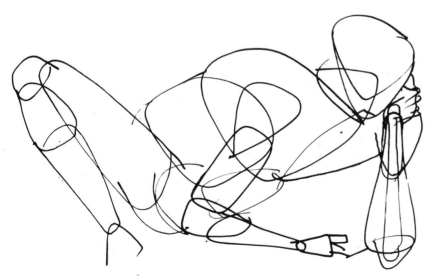

Analysis of Schnabel's Drawing

David Green, *Fledglings,* **charcoal, 17" x 11" (43 x 28 cm)**

Chapter 6

Design

and

Composition

Beauty is truth; truth, beauty.
John Keats

IN ART EDUCATION the terms design and composition, through common usage, have become interchangeable without necessarily being synonymous. The student-artist, therefore, is denied the opportunity to question and reasonably distinguish between the practical and definable factors involved in spatial organization, *COMPOSITION,* and the intangible, aesthetic, creative constituents through which the intent or purpose, *DESIGN,* is realized. Regardless of terminology, much of the aesthetic and expressive element of visual art escapes satisfactory definition. On the other hand, there exist proven visual and psychological devices through which artists realize their own vision. The demonstrations, examples and exercises presented in this and the next chapters are meant for that purpose.

For the sake of clarity we shall think of composition as the means through which design is realized. For example, the card displaying the words *Hot Dogs* is *composed* of a horizontally placed white rectangle containing a black rectangle interspersed with cursive and linear accents (the letters) *designed* to sell hot dogs.

HOT DOGS

Content

The true content of visual art is not necessarily the recognizable subject realistically represented on the picture plane. The expressive and aesthetic potentials of design in drawing, painting or print are dependent on the spatial allotment and organization of its elements. This is true regardless of the subject or title. To clarify this concept imagine yourself as a journalistic photographer, assigned to illustrate a magazine article on the geological features of the American Southwest. The article stresses the dominating presence of *space* and the *monumental* formations that occupy it. You decide, therefore, that the motivating theme for your assignment is to capture and convey to the viewer the essence of space and monumentality.

**Sketch of Three Landscapes Demonstrates Space and
Monumentality with Linear Diagrams**

After surveying the landscape, you select an isolated butte as your objective, *a.* An experienced artist, you climb to the top of the formation, manipulate the viewfinder of your camera until the horizon line extends near the top of the picture plane. Then either by elevating or lowering the angle of the lens, a prominent projection rises above the horizon line and you snap the shutter. The result, *b,* is an impression of *space.* Later you descend to a position near the base of the formation and angle the lens upward until a triangular shaped projection seems to slice diagonally across the upper area of the picture plane. The result is an impression of *monumentality, c.* The recognizable subject in each picture is a rock formation; however, the true con-tent is *space* and *monumentality,* two abstract, universal factors that have been included as thematic material in literature and music as well as visual art. The accompanying diagrams are linear abstractions of the spatial organization (composition) of each design. The true content or hidden subject of each version was achieved through a visual device generally referred to as the point of view.

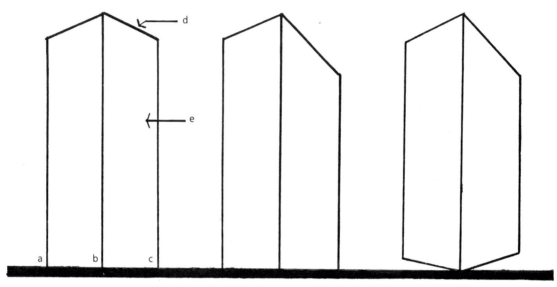

Diagram of the Angle in Spatial Organization

Point of View

When reading a screenplay one notices frequent notations—P.O.V.—indicating that a specific viewpoint is recommended. By stressing the *point of view,* the screenwriter and director are taking advantage of one of the most important factors in graphic design. The persuasive potential of point of view originates in our instinct for survival, our need to determine the position of objects in space relative to our own. Photography depends on the position and angle of the camera lens. Visual art is conceived through a linear organization of the picture plane in which angles, acute and obtuse, play important roles.

The effectiveness of the angle in spatial organization is demonstrated in the diagram. The vertical lines *A, B,* and *C* are equally spaced in each diagram. By increasing the slope of the angle *D* in the second and third diagrams, the area of plane *E* seems to increase. The bottoms of the first two diagrams are shown at eye level. However, upward angles drawn from the medial point of the third diagram not only raise the eye level but also increase the distance between the subject and the viewer.

Interiors

The dramatic effect gained by representing a subject within an interior has been appreciated and utilized extensively in visual art. The diagrams of interiors demonstrate four points of view. The viewer is *positioned* below the subject in *a*. In *b* the view is from above. In *c* the subject is seen from the left, and in *d* from the right.

Joseph Mugnaini, *The Prelate,* **intaglio, 11" x 15" (28 x 38 cm), with grid**

The Grid System

The first requirement for achieving meaningful spatial composition is that the immediacy of the picture plane must be recognized and appropriately exploited. A graphic device that has proven helpful for that purpose is the *grid system,* a method founded on the following concepts:

1. During the initial stage of spatial organization neither form nor space, as indicated on the picture plane, is granted priority.

2. Within the limited area of the picture plane both are considered to be equally important and at all times independent.

3. In the beginning or exploring stage the element of line neither surrounds nor separates form from space.

The figure in the intaglio, for example, was suggested by the triangle indicated at the left of center of the accompanying grid. At that beginning stage either the triangle or its environment could have suggested any number of subjects without disturbing the original spatial arrangement suggested by the grid.

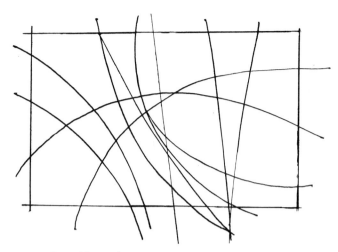

Doodle for Grid Exercise

An effective, adaptable procedure for implementing a workable grid coincides with an inherent human ability to sense harmonious proportion, rhythm and consistency in form and motion in space. Many of us doodle, an unconscious act in which a pointed device, which could be anything from a finger to a stick, pencil or pen, is activated to perform rhythmic dancelike markings on a responsive surface. The results are often surprisingly satisfying for they are performed without anxiety while the mind and often the eye are preoccupied. The following exercise is designed to convert a normally dormant talent so often evident in a doodle to practical use.

EXERCISE

You will need a pencil or pen and several sheets of paper, any size, to complete the exercise.

1. First sketch a rectangle to represent the picture plane. A horizontally placed rectangle is recommended for the first trial.

2. With free continuous sweeping motions, slice and swing with pen or pencil, across, downward, upward and *beyond* the borders of the picture plane. Each stroke should be completed with a follow-through motion comparable to the stroke of a golfer or the swing of a baseball bat that continues after the moment of impact. The grid should be completed within a few seconds. An example is shown.

3. Establish a pattern within the grid by filling in with tone every other intersected area, making certain that no areas with tone are adjacent to each other. In this case tone represents solidity or form. The result should resemble the first version of the development of the doodle.

4. Trace the original grid established in step 2 on a separate sheet of paper and reverse the order of step 3 by filling in with tone the areas that previously were left untouched.

Development of the Doodle, First Version

Development of the Doodle, Second Version

William Blake, *The Great Red Dragon and the Woman Clothed with the Sun,* watercolor, National Gallery of Art, Washington, Rosenwald Collection, with grid diagram

The exercise demonstrates the importance of rhythm and proportion in spatial composition and the inseparable relationship between form and space as depicted on the restricted area of the picture plane. It is not unreasonable to conclude that many recognized works of art originated with a sophisticated doodle. Consider, for example, the illustration by William Blake. The accompanying diagram reveals the dynamic, rhythmic linear pattern underlying the design.

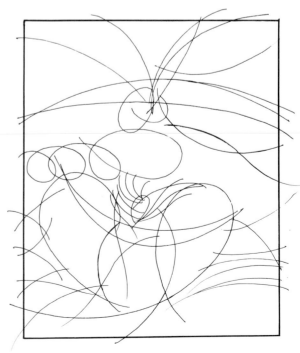

Joseph Mugnaini, *Lunar Blossom,* **pen and ink, 7" x 10" (18 x 25.5 cm), with grid diagram**

The pen and wash drawing, *Lunar Blossom,* is based on a series of intersecting sweeping curves and loops, generally contained within the central area of the picture plane. Solidity is represented by light values; however, the tonal pattern could have been reversed without affecting either the linear dynamics or the interlocking shapes of the composition shown in the accompanying diagram.

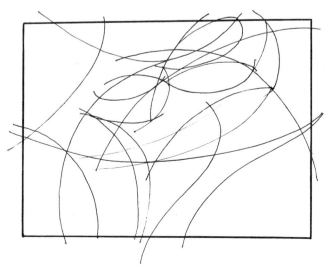

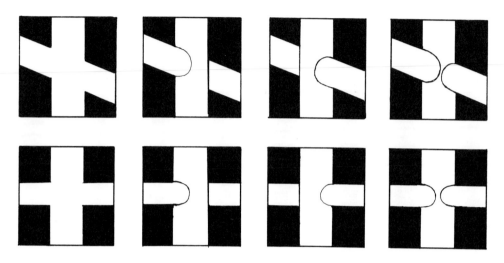

The Arc and the Angle

The problem of either foreshortening form or representing it in space relative to the viewer is solved by adding an *arc* to the angle. The simple, yet infallible method of controlling the viewpoint is demonstrated in the crossbar diagram. A minimal rearrangement of two factors, a short linear thrust and an arc (half a circle), radically alters the viewpoint. Two silhouetted images are shown, one with an obliquely placed crossbar (top), and one with a horizontally placed crossbar (bottom). In the first panel of each version the image is flat and two-dimensional. In the top second panel the addition of an arc on the left side of the vertical bar and a linear thrust on its right side raises the crossbar above eye level. In the third panel the crossbar is placed below eye level by reversing the positions of the arc and the linear thrust on the vertical bar. In the fourth panel two arcs together in the middle of the vertical bar not only place the connection at eye level, but also bring the extensions closer together to form a right angle. In the bottom image, the horizontal crossbar is rotated to the right or left depending on the position of the arcs and linear thrusts on the vertical base. (The thrust is essentially a continuation of the edge of the bar opposite to the arc.)

The same principle of repositioning arcs and linear thrusts can be applied to other subjects. The first stage of the tree diagrams is presented as a flat outlined form. In the next two versions its limbs and branches are relocated by alternating or reversing the positions of the arc and linear thrust on the main trunk.

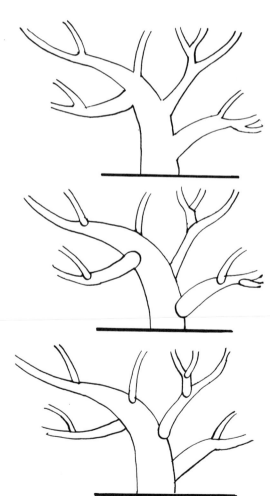

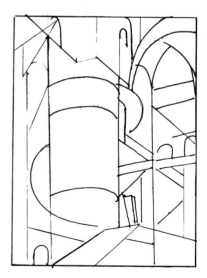

Facsimile of a Preliminary Study for an Etching by Giovanni Piranesi for *Le Carceri* with Diagram

The arc and the angle have been fully employed in Giovanni Piranesi's preliminary sketch for one of a series of etchings, *Le Carceri* (*The Prisons*). The picture plane has been organized to place the viewer within an interior of indefinite dimensions where he or she is confronted and surrounded by arches, vaults, buttresses, staircases and columns that extend above, below, to the left, right and behind. The accompanying diagram shows the spatial arrangement of the arcs and angles used in the composition.

The preliminary sketch for a major work by Luca Cambiasco reveals a definite understanding of the dramatic potential that may be gained by controlling the point of view in spatial design. The *arcs* and the *linear thrusts* that define the *angle* have been skillfully adapted to place grouped images above, below and to the right of the viewer. The eye-level viewpoint is located in the center of the design. Deep space is implied by overlapping the smaller figures in the background, elevating the larger equestrian figure toward the upper region of the picture plane and foreshortening the figure lying on its back near the foreground. The accompanying diagram demonstrates the basic linear concept for the design in which the arc, combined with the angle, plays a major role.

Luca Cambiasco, *Martyrdom of Saint Lawrence,* **pen and brown ink with brown wash, 15¼" x 9⅝", National Gallery of Art, Washington, Ailsa Mellon Bruce Fund, with diagram**

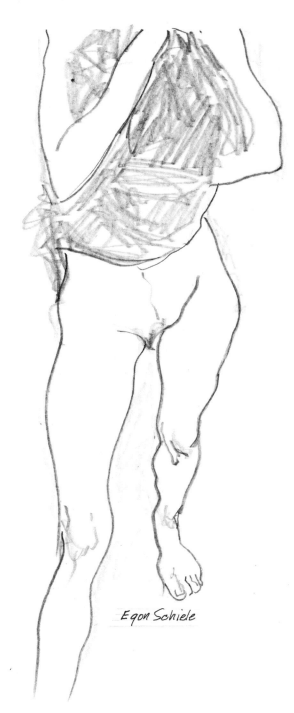

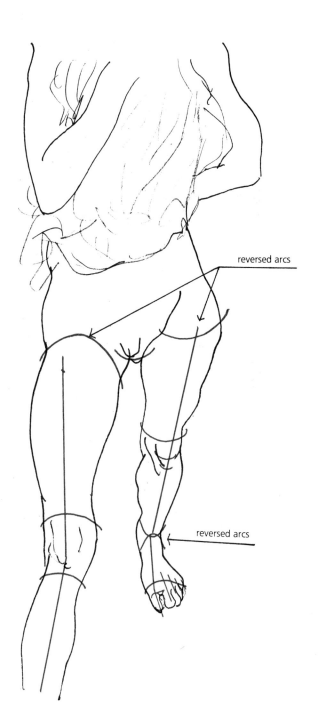

reversed arcs

reversed arcs

Pencil Facsimilie of a Drawing by Egon Schiele with Diagram of Arcs and Angles

The exaggerated angles of the legs in Egon Schiele's drawing were made believable by conceiving their spatial positions with the hidden arcs shown in the diagram. The clue to the approach is in the arclike detail of the subject's left kneejoint.

Chapter 7

Drawing

Concepts

Artistic growth is, more than it is anything else,
a refining of the sense of truthfulness. The stupid
believe that to be truthful is easy. Only the artist,
the great artist, knows how difficult it is.
Willa Sibert Cather

A DRAWING STYLE and the means for developing it
vary with the individual, yet the technique through
which style is recognized either follows or is based on one
of a number of universally accepted approaches. In this
chapter five methods that have prevailed in creative,
expressive drawings and graphics are reviewed and
demonstrated: contained form, contour, action, calligraphic and crosshatch drawing. A working acquaintance
with each should control a natural urge to *acquire* a style
prematurely before developing one's own. It would be an
oversimplification to state that within these approaches the
student-artist will eventually *discover* a style that seems to
conform to his or her needs. It is not a matter of sampling,
comparing and selecting a suitable idiom. Ironically, it is the
gifted student who seems most vulnerable to a temptation
to settle for expediency in place of serious study, cleverness
instead of reason, and to mistake novelty for originality. A
technique or style should be allowed to grow from within
during an extended period of observation, analysis and
practice. During periods of experimentation and study the
student should maintain a neutral attitude toward style,
keeping in mind that practical and intuitive factors involved
in art may be combined effectively only through varied
experiences, and that *specialization* arrests progress.

Approach each exercise with a clear understanding of the
scope of the exercise, the medium to be used and the time
span in which it is to be developed. The technique adopted
by runners competing in different events where energy and
speed are equated with space and time would be much the
same. The long-distance runner, like the sprinter, must conform to natural laws and man-made rules. Each must expend
energy in coordination with a *pace* calculated to cover efficiently a predetermined distance within an allotted span of
time. Neither runner would consider exchanging preestablished paces during a race. The long-distance runner, by
accelerating his pace, would soon collapse; the sprinter, by
decreasing his, would lag behind his competitors.

Rembrandt, *Jan Cornelius Sylvius,* **pen and bistre, 5¹/₄" x 4⁴/₅" (13.5 x 12 cm), National Gallery of Art, Washington, Rosenwald Collection**

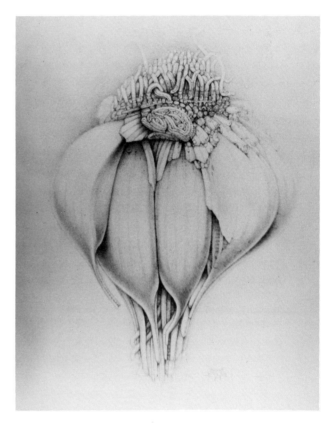

Robert Weaver, *Head of Garlic,* **pencil, 7¹/₂" x 10" (19 x 25.5 cm)**

Consistency of attitude and technique has been the hallmark of style in most human enterprises, including the arts. In *Jan Cornelius Sylvius* by Rembrandt the spirited energy of an action drawing, like a sprint race, was developed directly within a limited area in a brief span of time.

In *Head of Garlic* by Robert Weaver, however, the drawing was gradually evolved through several stages over an extended period of time. In each case a predetermined pace and concept were maintained.

The exercises presented in the next five sections should all be executed with the element of line.

Contained Form Drawing

Contained form drawing is an approach in which a subject is reduced to a compact geometric shape. The best-known examples are in Pre-Columbian sculpture. The attraction of contained form is derived from its *primary* shape, which in plastic art may be a cube, sphere, oval, pyramid, cone and so on. In visual art the primary shape could be a rectangle, circle, ellipse, triangle and the like. The formula for a contained form drawing is based on developing an image in approximately three stages without diminishing the visual impact of the primary shape.

1. The primary shape is established.

2. Secondary shapes are developed that either harmonize with or complement the primary shape.

3. Tertiary or subsidiary shapes are added that are designed to be consistent with the first and second state of the drawing.

The attractive, powerful imagery of contained form is exemplified here in four contemporary pieces. *Ramona* is a drawing contained within a triangle. *Presentiment* is a bronze sculpture contained within an elongated cube. The composite drawing representing Pre-Columbian bas-reliefs, paintings and sculpture is another example of contained form. *Mana Nesian,* a carved model for a larger project, is contained within a cube.

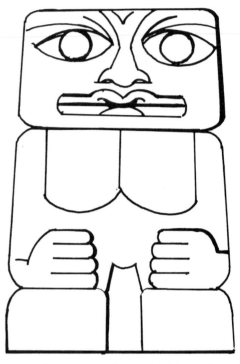

Composite Drawing of Pre-Columbian Sculpture

William Harmas, *Mana Nesian,* **carved clay**

Paul Kolosvary, *Ramona,* **graphite on hand-textured matte finish glass, 24¹/₂″ x 18¹/₂″ (62 x 47 cm)**

Charna Rickey, *Presentiment,* **polished bronze, 6¹/₂″ x 12″ x 5″ (16.5 x 30.5 x 12.5 cm)**

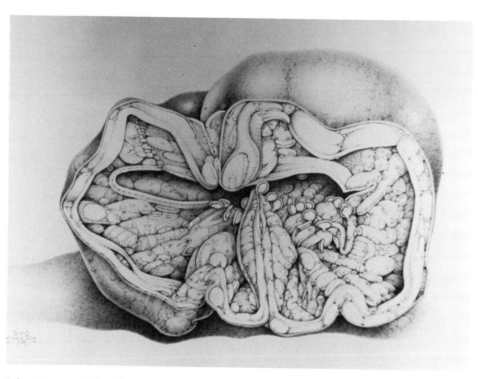

Robert Weaver, *Halved Tomato,* **pencil, 7¹/₂″ x 10″ (19 x 25.5 cm)**

Lenius Jorgensen, *Big Tim,* **etching, 9″ x 12″ (23 x 30.5 cm)**

The effectiveness of detail often relies upon spatial organization based upon contained shapes. With inventive skill, Robert Weaver has reduced the oval of a halved tomato to a rectangular primary shape. The secondary pattern, like a spiderweb, radiates from a point near the top central region of the rectangle to contain the smaller, subsidiary forms, which in turn conform to the radial symmetry introduced in the secondary pattern.

The primary shape in the etching by Lenius Jorgensen is an irregular black parallelogram that surrounds a hidden parallelogram suggested by the extremities of the limbs of the subject. The subsidiary shapes are arranged to conform with the oval-shaped shell and the rectangular limbs of the tortoise.

Jean Ingres, *Thomas Church, 1816,* **graphite, 7³/₈" x 6¹/₄", Los Angeles County Museum of Art, Laula D. Lasker Estate Fund 1967**

The distinct, compact, often monumental imagery of contained form design is frequently confused with compositional devices such as the triangle, oval, circle and rectangle. Geometric devices have served as a basis for infinite variations in spatial composition. The key word is *basis,* a term with a meaning different from the term *containment.* The difference becomes evident when the works of Ben Shahn and Jean Ingres are compared. The brush and ink drawing by Ben Shahn is totally *contained* within a rectangle. The drawing by Ingres is partially contained and partially supported by a triangle. In other words, a triangle forms a *basic* framework supporting elements of the subject that, at various points, project beyond its triangular limits.

Ben Shahn, *Dr. J. Robert Oppenheimer,* **brush and ink, 19¹/₂" x 12¹/₄" (49.5 x 31 cm), The Museum of Modern Art, New York**

Diagram of Crouching Model in Three Stages

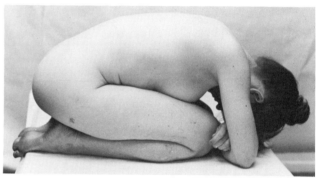

Model in Crouched Position

The crouching position assumed by the model in the photograph is frequently used for classroom exercises in drawing contained shapes. A typical approach is shown in three stages in the accompanying diagram. In the first stage the subject is reduced to a simple geometric shape, comparable to the primary shape in contained sculpture. This reduction is usually accomplished with one area-encompassing stroke such as inscribing a closed letter of the alphabet. Next the areas occupied by the limbs and torso in this position are roughly indicated with free slicing strokes. These are secondary shapes designed to harmonize with the primary area. The subsidiary shapes are added in turn to harmonize with the secondary shapes.

Some poses are best reduced to a primary shape by overlapping two of their prominent features. The compact position of the seated model shown in the photograph was unified by a student in three stages. First the rectangular combination of shoulders and arms is overlapped with a rough triangle formed by the pelvis, thighs and legs. In the second phase the general structure, proportions and positions of the arms and legs are introduced as secondary shapes consistent with, and in harmony with, the primary shape formed by the rectangle and the triangle. Subsidiary detail completes a basis for a finished drawing.

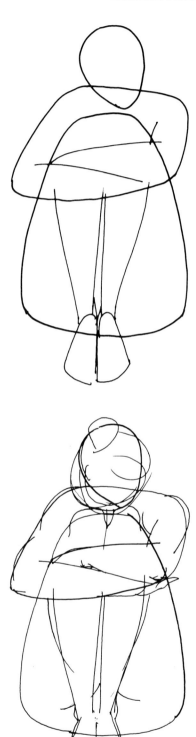

Model in Compact Position

Diagram of Compact Position in Three Stages

Contour Drawing

Contour drawing involves more than just separating an object from space with a carefully rendered line. The first drawings by children and work produced by pre-historic and primitive societies are prompted by an inherent method of visual communication in which the element of line is used either exclusively, or as a dominant factor.

There are two recognized contouring methods: point-to-point contour drawing and continuous contour drawing.

The *point-to-point* approach requires a free motion of the drawing instrument upon the surface of the picture plane, moved in a direct, uninhibited manner from one prese-lected point to another. The drawing is completed through a series of fairly straight and curvilinear strokes based upon understanding the structure of the subject as well as its highly visible edges. Raul Dufy demonstrates a free point-to-point calligraphic technique where the various pressures and speeds involved in the development of the drawing are permanently registered as well as the linear image of the woman. This is a direct approach where consistency of motion, rhythm and the time or speed involved in each stroke are as essential to its content as the subject.

In contrast, Aubrey Beardsley displays a *continuous contour*. This method requires a carefully planned composition that is later rendered in a continuous, gradually developed line. Variations in its linear design are carefully planned and maintained. Calligraphy is absent. Continuous contour is an indirect approach in which the drawing is completed through several stages. The element of time involved in its development is not evident. Any indication of calligraphy would be inconsistent with its design.

Beside each drawing is a hypothetical example of a pear as it would be conceived by either Dufy or Beardsley.

Every stroke of a well-conceived, well-executed contour drawing is founded on familiarity with the structure, volume and planes that determine the silhouette or outline of the subject. It is a knowledge gained through concerted study and practical experience. The freely applied strokes of a point-to-point drawing are a continuing series of sensitive

Facsimilie Drawing after Raul Dufy with Pear

responses to subtle rhythms and harmonious proportions stimulated by the total reality of the subject, not only by its edges. A slow-motion film of a well-conceived and skillfully executed stroke in a point-to-point contour drawing would show that it begins by retaining some of the character and quality of the previous stroke. As the stroke develops it not only predicts where it will terminate but also hints at the character and quality of the following stroke. It also maintains the imagery or style of the artist who activates it.

The linear dynamics of a contour drawing rely greatly on accents and variations in the weight or thickness of line. These are qualities realized through various speeds and pressures of the instrument or medium at the point of contact, especially in point-to-point contour drawing. In this method sight and touch are coordinated to sense and relate the quality of line to the relative flexibility of a pen or the rigidity of a pencil. By increasing or decreasing the tension at the point of contact while the instrument is in motion, one is able to feel as well as see the graphic quality of a line and its relationship to the total design. In contour drawing, as in action drawing, the picture plane may be compared to a piano keyboard that is manually activated with spatial movements of the arms and hands, coordinated with the sense of touch—an act that can be performed with eyes closed.

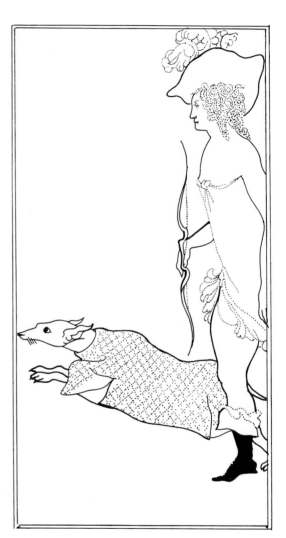

Facsimilie Drawing after Aubrey Beardsley with Pear

Essentially, a point-to-point contour drawing is composed of a series of coordinated interconnected lines and curves that are *pulled* from one designated point to another. A typical example in figure drawing could be a long arc originating at a point near the great trochanter and terminating at a point slightly above the knee; or it could be a short deep arc describing the contour of the deltoid muscles of the arm. The number of movements required to complete a passage or segment of the design depends upon the artist. One might use a compound motion to describe a particular form while another might interpret it with two or even three movements. The *pulling* experience may be understood through an exercise in which the tension or pressure of the instrument at the point of contact is conceived as the focal point where the sense of sight and touch are simultaneously unified in the act of contour drawing.

EXERCISE

You will need the following equipment and materials:

1. A stick, branch or length of bamboo at least three feet long and about one inch in diameter at its thickest end, tapering to about one-quarter inch at the tip. The tip may be shaped to function like the nib of a pen.

2. A small wide-mouthed container to hold at least one inch of ink.

3. A bottle of india ink.

4. Several sheets of paper at least 22" x 30" (56 x 76 cm) and either a drawing board or piece of masonite large enough to support the paper.

The purpose of the exercise is to provide an experience with a special instrument that may be transferred or subconsciously carried over to other instruments like a pencil, pen, crayon, charcoal and brush. The process is simple and direct.

1. Secure the paper to the board, lay it flat on the floor, pick up the stick or branch and assume a standing position near the bottom of the drawing board.

2. Like a fencing master, with arm extended hold the point of the stick, rapierlike, near the upper region of the paper. This will be the starting point of a preconceived stroke.

3. Dip the point in the ink, swing it to the starting area and imagine a line to be drawn from that point to another near the bottom of the paper. Press the point firmly on the surface. This will result in tension at the point of contact that must be maintained throughout the stroke.

4. With your arm extended and maintained in a rigid position and your feet slightly parted, pull the point toward you with a firm steady motion that involves the weight and controlled action of your body as well as your arm. Imagine that the stroke, if continued beyond the edge of the paper, would end somewhere between or near your feet. While pulling the line, you may need to lean backward, shift weight from one foot to the other or even relocate your position to the right or left of the drawing board. These adjustments are usually instinctively made during the act. The resulting line will be incisive and sharp, the graphic artifact of an uninhibited motion.

5. Repeat the process, including several trials with eyes shut. You will soon be aware that using an instrument such as a long stick forces you to pull the line. There is no alternative; only a moderate lateral motion is permitted.

By coordinating arm and body action with stances or positions that are compatible with each motion, the options of creative and expressive *point-to-point* drawing are infinite.

At this point, try other linear configurations, cursive, curvilinear, long and short arcs and so on.

6. To continue the exercise, place the board on an easel at a vertical or semivertical angle. Maintaining the extended arm and stick position, repeat the movements. Keep in mind during the process both the tactile and perceptive sensations that were experienced with the picture plane in its previous position. You will soon adjust to the vertical angle.

7. Select a subject to work from (a model, clothed or draped, a bottle, a still life, a landscape) and interpret it through a point-to-point contour drawing.

8. Finally, abandon the stick. With the remembered movements draw the same object or subject with different instruments: a pen, a pencil, charcoal, conte crayon and a brush.

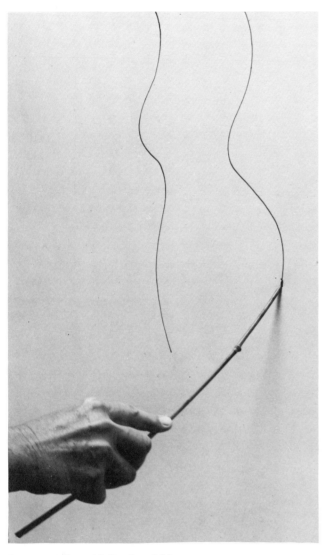

Demonstration with Bamboo Stick

Gene Hackman, *Contour Study, Using Bamboo Stick, of Female Figure,* **18"x 40" (46 x 101.5 cm)**

The purpose of an experiment, study or exercise is either to overcome a specific problem, to understand an elusive concept or to acquire a special skill. In the field of music a student may turn to mathematics to study harmony and counterpoint. In athletics the boxer punches a bag to improve coordination. The swimmer runs long distances to improve stamina. In our exercise the purpose is to emphasize the importance of the sense of touch and how it is directly involved in the analytical, creative and expressive aspects of drawing. It is also meant to provide an experience that may be carried over and incorporated, in varying degrees, with other drawing concepts and approaches.

The photographed demonstration with the board in a vertical position shows a cursive downward stroke being developed with a bamboo stick. Notice the tension originating at the point of contact and extending through the bowed stick to the hand.

The contour study of the female figure in profile was completed within a period of fifteen minutes. The paper was firmly fastened to a drawing board in a vertical position on an easel. The instrument used was a bamboo stick similar to the one shown in the photograph.

The graphic eloquence of a brush drawing is evident in the serigraph by Robert Brown. In this case the nagging problem of developing a clean opaque white line on a black surface was solved through an indirect method. The original brush and ink drawing was transferred to a silk screen plate through photoprocessing, then reproduced as a print. It is an exceptional example of point-to-point contour drawing, skillfully and sensitively orchestrated with a variety of pressures, speeds and directions of the brush while in motion.

The pen and wash figure by Marie Starr is a continuous contour drawing. She used a no. 5 round-point Speedball pen to produce a line of constant thickness regardless of the direction of the stroke. The time element in a drawing of this type has little bearing on the result. The concept is based on an *indirect* approach that requires several stages for completion. Lines may be reworked, contours altered and detail added. The artist selected the freely applied strokes of various thickness, representing the drapery, to counteract the lithesome continuous outline of the subject. The instrument chosen to achieve the active, incisive linear pattern of the drapery is a no. 5 chisel-point Speedball pen. She applied the middle tone wash with a two-inch sable brush. The accompanying diagram demonstrates in detail how the volumes and planes of the subject are suggested by short linear excursions or projections away from the main contour, directed toward the interior area of the figure.

Robert Brown, *Seated Figure,* **serigraph**

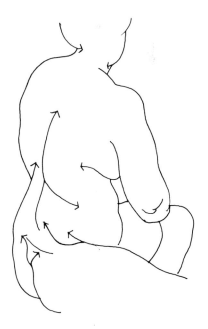

Marie Starr, *Novella,* **pen and wash, 18" x 25" (46 x 63.5 cm),
with diagram**

The eloquence of simplicity is exemplified in the contour drawing by a master draftsman. With a few shrewdly selected strokes, Edward Reep presents a whimsical interpretation of a pose, prompted by the incongruous spectacle of a nude with a hat, holding a cigarette. With the exception of the detailed hands, head and hat, the drawing was completed with approximately a dozen strokes.

Nasturtiums by Janice Loovis is an example of a line and wash drawing carefully and deliberately rendered over a considerable period of time. The subject, unlike the human figure, landscape or assembled still life, is not conducive to the contour drawing approach. Free stroking is absent. The spatial arrangement of the subject's components discourages contained or compact composition. The radiating, twisting dancelike image was achieved through several stages in which the direction and quality of line were surveyed and adjusted to attain the planned effect.

Study of a Seated Girl by Al Johnson is an exercise in which the sides, edges and tips of a lozenge or cube-shaped conte crayon are quickly and expertly administered. The strokes, predominately curvilinear, are arranged in a swinging circular pattern that carry the eye from the edges of the image toward a point near the hands.

Edward Reep, *Nude with a Hat and Cigarette,* pen and ink

Janice Loovis, *Nasturtiums,* **line and wash**

Al Johnson, *Study of a Seated Girl,* **conte crayon, 18" x 22" (46 x 56 cm)**

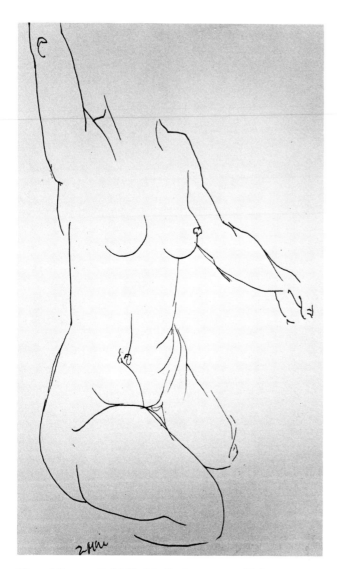

Vincent Rascon, *Quick Sketch, Contour,* **pen and ink**

Vincent Rascon, *Quick Sketch, Contour,* **pen and ink**

The special quality or uniqueness of a medium can be experienced and appreciated by comparing it with another while being engaged in a similar project under like circumstances. Here we compare a wet medium administered with a pointed instrument to one in which both instrument and medium are dry and self-contained. The four quick contour sketches that follow were especially completed for this book by two excellent draftsmen and artists who as teachers specialize in figure drawing. The subject is the female figure. The objective is to demonstrate a point-to-point quick sketch of either the front, side or back of the figure with emphasis on the torso.

Each of the two point-to-point contour sketches by Vincent Rascon were completed within two minutes. The sharply defined strokes were produced with a no. 6 Speedball pen. During the process the position and character of each stroke were briefly contemplated, then quickly applied with a positive motion of the pen. The same degree of pressure and the same rate of speed were applied to each stroke, whether long, short or curved. After each stroke the pen was lifted for a moment while the following stroke was being considered, then lowered to repeat the process. The result is a circulating, staccato movement with short pauses suggested where the strokes are not quite connected.

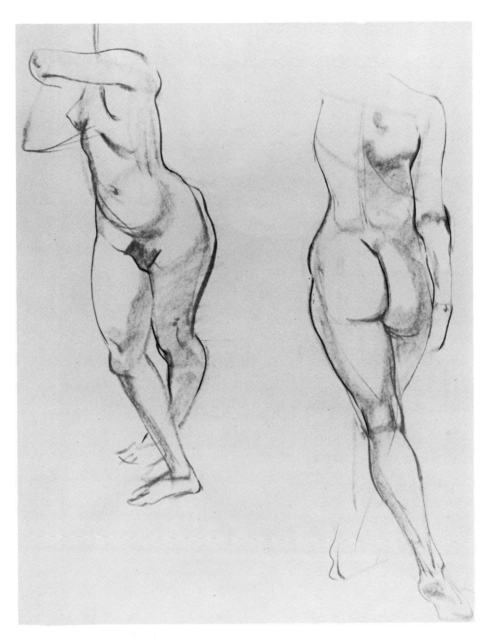

Victor Casados, *Quick Sketch, Contour,* **conte crayon**

The two studies by Victor Casados are remarkable examples of skillful manipulation of a faceted, cubelike crayon. He chose NuPastel, which embodies the dry blacks of charcoal and the semidry quality of conte crayon. The flowing harmonious variations in the thickness of line and values of tone were made possible by contacting the surface of the paper with the planes, edges and tips of the crayon in motion. The images are based upon both the point-to-

point and continuous contour approaches. This can be seen in the sweeping curves that describe the pelvic contours and the thighs. Essentially they are continuous, yet the points that indicate the location of the crest of the ilium, the great trochanter and the origin and terminus of the muscles of the thigh are distinctly accented. The time required for each sketch was three minutes.

Action Drawing

Action drawing is not necessarily an approach in which action or dynamics of motion is represented. Its subject could be either abstract or a theme based on the stable shapes of a range of mountains. The attraction of an action drawing relies chiefly on the dynamics of activated line that induces the viewer to recapitulate the act through which it was developed. In many cases one is able to locate where the act began and where it ended. Contemporary art has been credited for originating action drawing and painting, yet the animated sketches by Rembrandt, Goya and other artists of the past are remarkable achievements in action drawing comparable to any produced today.

The title of David Starrett's drawing refers to a race, which of course involves action or motion. However, it is the manner in which he activated the pen within the area and on the surface of the paper that makes it an action drawing. In action drawing the artist can feel the wetness of the ink or wash flowing into the textured surface of paper or the dryness of crayon or charcoal impregnating with black the white exposed areas of the picture plane. An *action drawing* is an artifact of an act, a graphic version of an emotional experience that may never be duplicated, not even by its creator.

Robert Chuey, *Old Man with a Cane,* **pen and ink**

David Starrett, *The Rat Race,* **pen and ink, 6" x 10" (15 x 25.5 cm)**

If *Old Man with a Cane* were completed with a round-pointed brush and black oil paint on a canvas covered with wet white oil pigment, it would be known as an action painting. Actually, it was sketched in less time than it took the ink to dry. The dark angular smears resulted from a final flick of the thumb over and across linear impressions that were still wet. The artist used a no. 5 chisel-point Speedball pen that was heavily loaded with black india ink. The jagged, wavering, vibrating character of the interwoven linear pattern results from two factors: The penholder was stubby, three inches long, gripped vertically with its top pressed in the center of the artist's palm; *strokes* were more or less scored or scratched on the surface, the *pulling* action was minimized. A work of this type is not meant as a study. It is the result of an intense reaction to a subject, object or event.

The running figure of a football player by Albert Porter is quickly stated with a continuous motion of the pen across the surface of the paper. One can almost hear the scraping of the point as it searches out the large contours of the back and the short, rapidly applied strokes indicating the position of the right arm.

In contrast, Gerald Brommer has indicated the structure of a building with sure, deliberate motions of a pen. In developing the sketch, the point was lifted from the surface after each stroke. The result is a staccato linear pattern based upon variations in architectural structure. Both drawings are active, linear *dances,* each exhibiting distinct rhythms suggested by the subjects.

Gerald Brommer, *Lucerne,* **pen and ink**

Albert Porter, *Football Player,* **pen and ink, 8" x 10" (20.5 x 25.5 cm)**

Peter Paul Rubens, *Venus Lamenting Adonis,* **drawing, 12" x 7⁴/₅" (30.5 x 20 cm), National Gallery of Art, Washington, Ailsa Mellon Bruce Fund, 1968**

Paul Kolosvary, *The Raincoat,* **stabile pencil and wash, 18³/₄" x 12¹/₂" (47.5 x 32 cm)**

The linear pattern of an action drawing usually does not feature or emphasize any specific part or element of a subject, including its contours. The movements involved are unpredictable, impulsive reactions to an imagined or perceived subject. There are exceptions when the contours of the subject are considered to be essential to its design. In that case, even though the rhythm and pace of the process is maintained, the action is controlled to delineate the con-

tours of the subject and separate it from the remainder of the picture plane. An example is in the study for a painting by Peter Paul Rubens, where the contour drawing approach has been combined with an action drawing.

Another example of a modified action drawing is in the free-spirited approach employed by Paul Kolosvary. The medium is a soft stabile pencil and wash.

The charcoal drawing by Harold Frank is an excellent example of *programmed* or *coded* action drawing. It essentially is an approach in which a preconceived pattern or grouping of strokes *automatically* is applied to a designated area. In this drawing it occurs on the left sides of the facial plane, the neck, and the shoulder of the subject, the areas of the picture plane surrounding the head and the upper region of the dress. The procedure is simple and direct. The pattern is preconceived; the charcoal is placed on the surface, strokes are applied, the charcoal is lifted and moved to another area where the process is repeated. The artist comments:

"In this drawing I use a thicker stick of charcoal. She was a delicious-looking woman and since I didn't want to get bogged down with belabored detail I worked with speed and sweep. My desire was to have the drawing have the look of a painting using the white of the paper like paint. I wanted to wed the subject to the background and the background to the subject so I invited one unto the other with speed—not as an intellectual or clinical device; rather as an emotional impetus. I wanted my drawing not to look pretty, yet even in my speed I cared and embraced it."

Harold Frank, *Head of Young Girl,* **crayon, 14" x 20" (35.5 x 51 cm)**

Linear Symmetry of Grass on a Hill and Scales on a Reptile

Calligraphic Drawing

Since the Renaissance, calligraphic drawing has been adopted as a shorthand method of gauging and describing two common, universally recurring patterns observed in the spatial and structural organization of both natural and man-made objects. For our purpose we shall refer to these as radial symmetry and linear symmetry. Patterns of *radial symmetry* are present in such unrelated objects as the eroded sides of a mountain, the spatial organization of plant life, the folds in drapery and the anatomy of animals. *Linear symmetry* reveals the spatial movement of such diverse subjects as a bristling field of corn, a patch of grass, a line of fence posts and the scaled flank of a reptile.

Calligraphic drawing differs from action or gesture drawing in its deliberate method of application. It is an approach derived from reflex action, comparable to experienced *pre-coded* acts like cutting a loaf of bread or hammering a nail. The technique involves two stages. First, the artist consciously appraises the subject and mentally reviews the movements required to represent it. Then, like writing a sentence, he or she proceeds to indicate graphically its basic spatial pattern.

The rhythmic symmetry of a rounded hill, *A,* an angular mountain, *B,* and the lower section of a tropical plant, *C,* have been quickly sketched with calligraphic drawing. Accompanying each sketch is a diagram of the first stage of each sketch in which the pattern was established without lifting the pen from the surface of the paper.

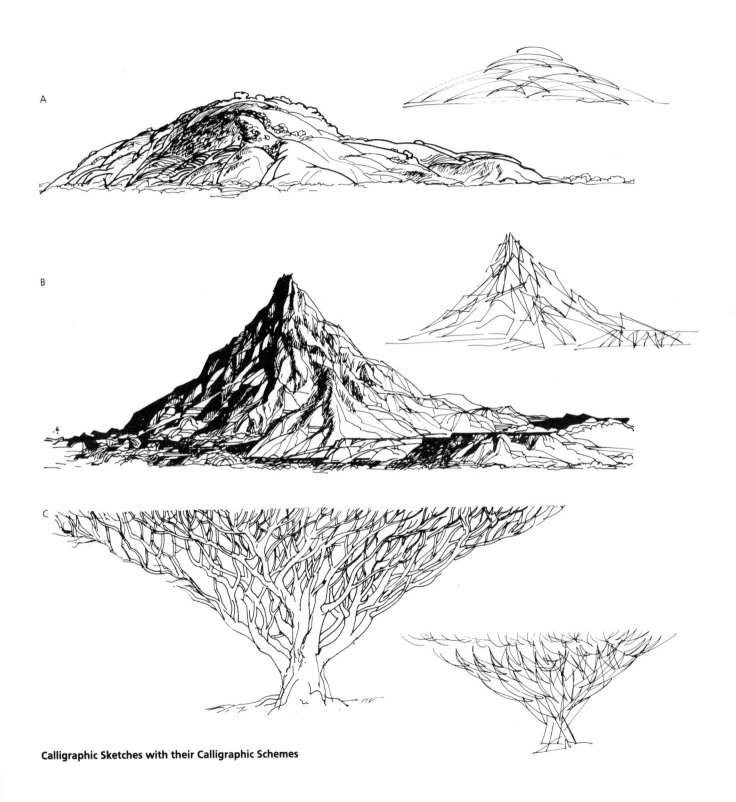

A

B

C

Calligraphic Sketches with their Calligraphic Schemes

**Andrew Wyeth, *Turkey Buzzard, Study from Life,* Courtesy
Museum of Fine Arts, Boston, Fund Mr. Karorik Bequest, with
diagram of radial linear symmetry.**

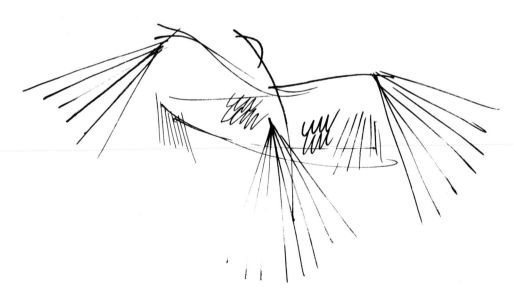

In many cases both radial and linear symmetry are combined, as in the wings and tail of Andrew Wyeth's *Turkey Buzzard*. Gauging and sensing the rhythm and consistency exhibited in radial and linear symmetry will help you to develop your own sense of rhythm and consistency, both essential factors in draftsmanship and spatial composition.

Spread your hand in an extended position. Notice that by drawing a series of thrusting lines radiating from a point slightly below your wrist and continuing through your extended fingers, you can quickly indicate the essential structure that governs the appearance not only of the human hand, but also the limb structure of the majority of animals that inhabit the earth.

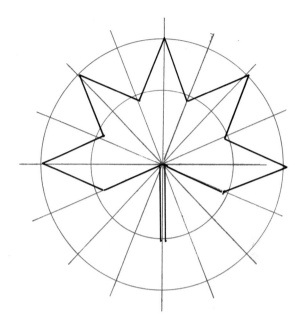

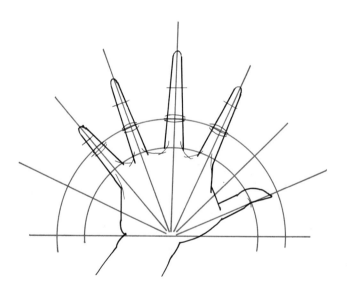

Diagram of Spread Hand

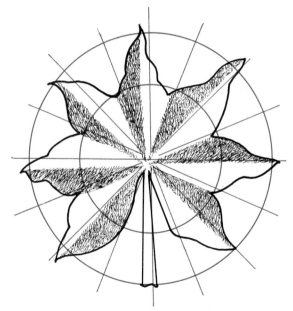

Supporting Structure in Flat Leaves and Drawing of Leaf

The supporting structure present in leaves with a flat, relatively large surface, is illustrated. Notice how the sharply delineated outline is the result of the radial thrusts of its skeletal supports.

Crosshatch Drawing

Hatch and crosshatch are techniques in which relatively short lines are drawn closely parallel to each other (the *hatch*), or across each other (the *crosshatch*). Both serve to develop tonal values and simulate the volumes, planes and contours of form. Before the invention of photoengraving, hatch and crosshatch lines were engraved or etched on wooden and metal plates used for book and newspaper illustration and reproductions of well-known paintings. Five basic hatch patterns are shown in the chart: the oblique, right angle and random crosshatch, and the curved and straight hatch.

In *Plant Study*, Gretel Stevens has *trapped* and shaped the meandering tip of a rose bush with random crosshatching.

Both the hatch and crosshatch have been skillfully adopted in *Doodles* by Peter Lasell. In the drawing on the left, the subject has been shaped from the outside with both the hatch and crosshatch. In the drawing on the right, the image has been developed as a vignette in which the volumes, planes and contours of the subject are modeled with a limited use of the hatch and crosshatch, combined with sharp-edged geometrically shaped blacks and a minimal use of line.

oblique
cross hatch

right angle
cross hatch

random
cross hatch

curved hatch

straight hatch

Five Basic Hatch Patterns

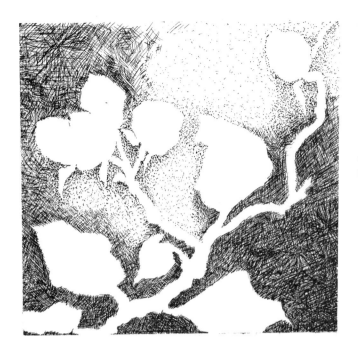

Gretel Stevens, *Plant Study,* **pen and ink, crosshatch, 5″ x 5¹/₄″ (12.5 x 13.5 cm)**

Peter Lasell, *Doodles,* **pen and ink, 9¹/₂″ x 8¹/₄″ (24 x 21 cm)**

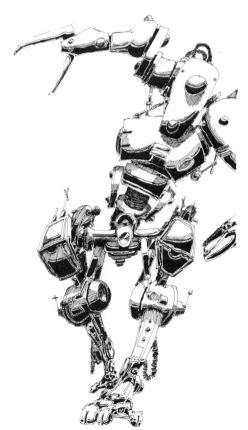

Sam Clayberger, *Seated Man,* **pen and ink**

Harry Wesslund, *Near Baden-Baden,* **pen and ink, 10" x 15" (25.5 x 38 cm)**

In *Seated Man,* Sam Clayberger modeled the faceted form of a clothed, seated figure with skillfully placed groupings of the *straight* hatch. This drawing exemplifies an approach where the pen is conceived as a chisel cutting into solid white marble. The volume and planes of the subject are suggested by varying the direction or angle of the strokes.

The shadows in *Near Baden-Baden* were realized with a closely stroked version of the *oblique* crosshatch. The roof was drawn with *straight* hatch groupings horizontally aligned with linear symmetry. The leaf masses of the tree were developed with a *random* crosshatch.

A prescribed approach toward developing a drawing on a white surface, especially with hatch and crosshatch methods, requires that the artist keep in mind that the area of whiteness as well as the intensity or purity of whiteness is limited. Like a sculptor beginning a project with a limited quantity of solid material who must carve space out of

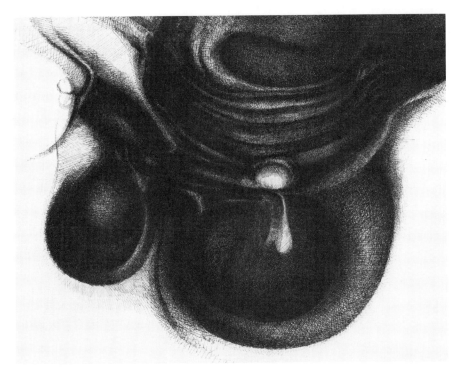

**Christine Taylor Patten, *Thirteen, 1975,*
pen and ink, 23" x 29"
Collection of Mr. and Mrs. G. D. Moore**

Barry Scharf, *Untitled,* pen and ink

solidity, the visual artist must adjust to the limited quantity and quality of whiteness offered by the picture plane (a sheet of paper) and be constantly aware of how it is being *spent.* During the development of a hatch or crosshatch tonal passage, the process should be conceived not as a method through which tone is applied to a white or light surface, but rather as a technique for shaping and controlling light or white values of the picture plane.

An excellent example of this approach is represented in the dark convoluted form in the drawing by Christine Taylor Patten. She designed a work in which the tonal values, ranging from black to white, were gradually evolved by applying tightly grouped strokes through which the underlying whiteness was, in varying degrees, *allowed to seep* through the controlled *transparency* of the crosshatch pattern. Without exception a well-executed crosshatch tonal area, regardless of its value, including a deep black, allows some of the underlying white value to be revealed between each stroke.

On many occasions the crosshatch is employed for limited or specific purposes. In the upper region of Barry Scharf's design, cloud formations, plant forms and terrain are suggested with a closely knitted hatch and crosshatch. In the lower region tonal variation and texture are depicted with a splattered pattern of dots superimposed over hatch strokes and loosely applied horizontal lines.

Chapter 8

Indirect

Drawing

In the field of
observation chance favors
the mind that is prepared.
Rene Vallery

INDIRECT DRAWING is an approach in which a work is developed through several stages. Usually the design is carefully planned for a continuing process that employs resists such as wax, rubber cement, glue, etc., for establishing a basic pattern. The design is further developed and carried toward completion by brushing, spraying or floating media over the pre-established resist pattern. Beside these traditional technique, electronic drawing is now possible using the computer (see page 193–197).

The Resist

The resist is a method for insulating areas of a surface either to be left untouched or to maintain preestablished values in areas scheduled for additional tonal development with a liquid medium. The resist may be either solid or liquid as long as it seals the surface of the work. In graphics, asphaltum, varnish, resin, and wax are used to protect areas of an etching plate from metal-eroding acids. For paper, the most popular and widely used resists have been paraffin, wax and crayon, but other materials such as linseed oil, glue and rubber cement have also been used.

Frisket

A dependable contemporary method is using a *frisket* masking medium that is available in two forms: sheets that can be precut and shaped with a razor blade or X-acto knife and a liquid that can be applied with an airbrush or conventional brush. A description of *frisket* as he used it on *The Train* is offered by the artist, Albert Porter:

Portraying power and energy were the main considerations in this free-spirited drawing of a steam locomotive. To achieve these qualities required an expressive use of line, first actively sought through liquid frisket lines on a heavy paper surface. Frisket, an art masking medium often used by watercolorists, can be easily applied with brushes (pre-soaped to protect the brush hairs), pen points or shaped sticks. Energizing the drawing with freely applied frisket

Albert Porter, *The Train,* pen, ink, frisket and wash, 9" x 12" (23 x 30.5 cm)

sets the mood for capturing the inside forces of steam loco-motion. After the frisket had dried, overwashes of ink were used to clarify the frisket line and suggest masses and implied background. When the frisket is rubbed off, finish-ing touches were made in ink with a pen. Drawings such as this one are helpful in building fluency for more deliberate work where explicit information is needed.

Aquatint

Aquatint is a process used to introduce tonal variations into an etching. Development requires several stages. In the initial stage either granulated or powdered acid-resisting resin is sprinkled on the surface of a copper or zinc plate. The plate is heated, causing the particles to form into tiny globules which adhere to the surface of the plate, leaving the exposed space between the particles vulnerable to the acid. Etching, inking and proofing the plate at this stage would produce an even-toned rectangular impression. At this point the surface of the plate may be compared to a sheet of paper ready for the application of a resist to preserve designated white or light patterns within a dark area of a design.

Here is a simplified version of the next stage as applied by Ettore Andreani in *Landscape*. The white areas surrounded by darks on the prepared surface of a zinc plate were brushed with a semi-liquid solution of asphaltum, which insulated the designated areas when the plate was immersed in acid. The acid eroded the exposed areas, thereby conditioning them to receive ink. Ink was rubbed into the eroded areas and the smooth surfaces were wiped clean. A sheet of paper was placed over the inked plate and rolled through a press, resulting in a print, an indirect method of producing a drawing. The equation is simple: *roughness* equals darkness; *smoothness* equals whiteness.

Ettore Andreani, *Landscape*, aquatint, 10" x 14" (25.5 x 35.5 cm)

Harry Sternberg, *Artists and Critics,* **woodcut**

Woodcut

Occasionally the medium used in a work of art may be mistaken for another, especially in the graphic arts. An etching may closely resemble a crosshatched pen and ink drawing or vice versa; a lithograph may be mistaken for a drawing done either with pen and ink, ink and wash or crayon. One medium seldom mistaken for another is the oldest of graphic media, the woodcut. The modern linoleum cut is also easily identified.

The woodcut is an excellent example of how the character of the medium is affected by the instrument or tool through which it is developed. The picture plane of a black-and-white woodcut, produced on a flat wooden surface, offers only one alternative to the artist, to introduce whiteness into a solid black area. This is accomplished by cutting emptiness into solidity, solidity representing black, emptiness, white. The instruments or tools for cutting range from pocket knives to specially designed chisels and gouges.

The eye-catching quality of a woodcut is basically rooted in two factors. First there is the extreme contrast in its tonal pattern. Middle values are practically absent, and only the lowest and highest values of the black-and-white version of the tonal scale are used. The second eye-catching characteristic is the impression of the *act* involved in cutting, gouging and slicing patterns into a moderately resistant three-dimensional surface.

Even though the design of *Artists and Critics* was not cut with conventional tools, the unique incisive character of the typical woodcut has been retained. The artist, Harry Sternberg, comments on the conceptual and technical aspects involved in its design:

I have worked most of this past year to produce a series of nine woodcuts, Myths and Rituals, *all done in black and white. For cutting I used a flexible shaft power tool with a variety of bits. No woodblock knives or gouges were used. I never do a detailed preparatory drawing for a print. I stain*

the block to a middle value with an ink wash and then do a *loose wash drawing in a darker value. As I begin cutting, the images slowly evolve and change, often in quite different directions from the starting concept. Since mistakes cannot be corrected on the block, this adventurous moving into unplanned changes is a thrilling adventure.*

In a traditional woodcut the incisive white accents impressed in the black areas are gouged or sliced with a chisel. The next two illustrations are examples of this sharply defined character of the woodcut being simulated with different mediums.

In *The* Kathleen *Deck Plan* the white accents surrounding the boat were shaped from the outside with a pen and brush by Rockwell Kent, one of the foremost wood engravers, illustrators and artists of our time.

In the relief print by Marty Mondrus acid was substituted for a chisel to erode depressions in a metal plate. These depressions are responsible for the white areas of *Self-Portrait.*

Marty Mondrus, *Self-Portrait,* relief etching

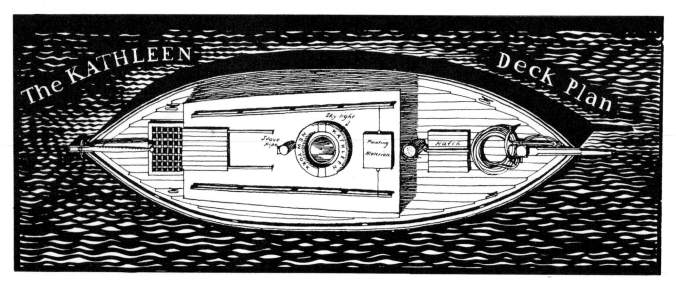

**Rockwell Kent, *The Kathleen Deck Plan,* pen and ink,
Collection of Irma and Mel David**

Serigraph

Serigraphy is a graphic method for producing a design with stencils. The *plate,* frequently referred to as a silk screen, is constructed by stretching a closely meshed length of silk over a wooden or metal frame. The frame is hinged to a solid, flat base in a manner which allows the silk at the bottom of the plate to completely contact the paper inserted underneath during the printing process. The frame, with silk at its bottom, forms a reservoir for a special dense ink that is squeezed with a rubber squeegee through the openings stenciled on the silk. The design is developed by blocking out areas of the screen with various types of resist such as torn or cut paper, liquid or solid touche or frisket, rubber cement, etc.

The serigraph, like the woodcut, lithograph, engraving or etching is an indirect method of drawing. Because of the thick pigmented inks used for reproducing the image, it is closely allied to painting.

In this serigraph the image of a seated woman has been reconstructed into an angular pattern. The element of line has been inadvertently introduced in the boundaries by the spatial arrangement of stencils used to develop the design. The absence of stroking by either pencil, brush or pen has been supplanted by visual evidence of tearing, cutting and *placement* of the stencils. The artist, Bettye A. Jaffe, comments:

I began this serigraph by doing a quick sketch of my mother. The paradox that we're permanently in transition has always excited me. I tried, by use of color and shapes, to express this constant change. The discovery that one does not paint with one's hands, but through the dictates of the unconscious was singularly freeing for me. Knowing that every time we start to create we must, of necessity, begin all over again, going back to the starting line, is both terrifying and thrilling. I think what really gave me my own voice was the realization that there is great beauty in imperfection.

Bettye A. Jaffe, *Seated Woman,* **serigraph, 18" x 24" (46 x 61 cm)**

Karl Hubenthal, *Seattle Slew,* **linecut/illustration, Courtesy of the Los Angeles** *Examiner*

Linecut

One of the most important contributions to modern publishing, especially in the field of journalism, is the development of a quick, inexpensive and reliable method for producing tonal values in *line cut* illustrations. In *Seattle Slew*, Karl Hubenthal has skillfully used the method. The procedure is technically simple. A crosshatched or dotted pattern, which is preprinted on transparent adhesive material, is pasted in areas where tonal values are required. The design is shaped with a sharp instrument and the unnecessary remnants are peeled off. The finished copy is photoengraved and printed. In this example the artist has added hatch strokes to emphasize the volumes, planes and detail of the subject.

Saul Bernstein, *Trotting Horse,* **computer**

The Computer

The most revolutionary instrument of recent time is the computer. With it, the elements of a design may be effort-lessly introduced to the picture plane, easily reviewed and instantly altered, combined, substituted or eliminated. It can add the element of motion, as shown in Saul Bern-stein's *Trotting Horse,* in a way formerly restricted to the field of film making.

Equipment for transmitting images from the hand of the artist to the screen of a computer varies with different models. At present there is a general tendency toward adopting the tablet and stylus system. The stylus is attached to the tablet, a portable rectangular panel, which in turn is connected to the computer. Within the tablet is a closely-meshed wire grid which is sensitive to the lightest

movement of the stylus on the surface of the tablet. The stylus, technically known as a *pen,* is equivent to a pencil; the tablet is comparable to a sketching pad.

During the development of an image the artist focuses on the screen where the design develops simultaneously with each stroke of the pen on the surface of the tablet. The visual elements are supplied through a pre-programmed *graphic menu* which is displayed on the screen with a touch of a button. Variations in line, tone, color and simu-lated texture are readily selected from the menu. Methods of applying the elements are also available through the menu. The strokes of a conventional brush, the airbrush, crosshatch, pen strokes and even glazing techniques are easily simulated with the pen and tablet. The potential for creative design is infinite.

Work completed on solid or opaque surfaces such as canvas, paper or plaster is perceived indirectly through light reflected from the pigmented surface of the picture plane. In contrast, the art of the computer screen is projected toward the viewer through beams of intense light generated within a television monitor. The medium is light itself. Color printers are on the market today that effectively reproduce on paper images created with a computer. However, the brilliant luminosity projected from the computer screen cannot, at present, be duplicated on either paper, canvas or any other surface.

The versatility of the computer is demonstrated in these two variations on a study for the figure of Adam by Michelangelo. One is rendered as a pen and ink sketch; the other is comparable to brush and ink combined with line drawn with a quill pen.

Saul Bernstein, *Adam*, variations on a study by Michelangelo. Courtesy the artist.

The portrait of Abraham Lincoln by Saul Bernstein was composed with letters forming words from Lincoln's Gettysburg address. The design is realized with three values: black, a middletone and white. The element of line, superimposed over the middletones, accents the facial features. Line is also used as a continuous contour to lend solidity and volume to the head.

A crosshatch over wash technique was used in the double portrait of the boxer Larry Holmes. Each drawing was completed with crosshatch strokes applied over a light value pattern selected from the menu. The tonal structure of the head at the left, above eye level, was deepened by superimposing additional strokes over a previously applied crosshatch pattern.

Saul Bernstein, *Portrait of Abraham Lincoln.* **Courtesy the artist.**

Saul Bernstein, *Portrait of Larry Holmes.*
Courtesy the artist.

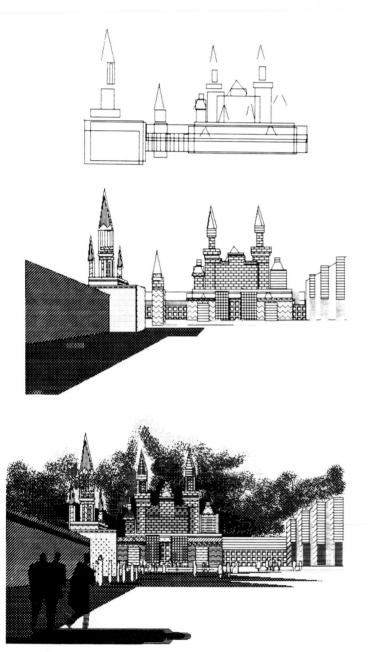

The nearly infallible capability of the computer as a drafting tool for indicating volume and space on a two dimensional surface with the elements of line and tone is remarkable. An example of the process is shown in three steps. The subject is a cityscape. First, the subject is outlined. Then, linear detail and tone are added. Finally, the sky is darkened to lend atmosphere to the design. Texture is suggested on the facade of the building near the middle of the composition. Darker figures are added, increasing the illusion of depth and space.

The Computer is an excellent tool for analyzing the structural elements of form regardless of the subject. An example is the human head which is one of the most demanding subjects in visual art. Its multifaceted appearance is at first confusing until it is reduced to its principal structural planes. Shown opposite is a simplified version of the planes as they are revealed by a computer with the light source located at various positions and angles.

The computer has simplified much of the technology of the film and television industry. Processes that required highly skilled technicians, lengthy periods of time and expensive laboratory equipment are now easily controlled by computers and a limited number of personnel. The potentials of the computer are still being explored and seem inexhaustible; yet the computer, like all media, has its limitations. It cannot initiate concepts or develop qualities in a design beyond the capability of its operator—in that regard it is no different from a pencil or pen. It is so far incapable of producing the sensual optical qualities provided by the textures and patinas of dry, wet, opaque and transparent media. Regardless of its shortcomings, however, the computer is destined to influence all fields of visual art. It is here to stay.

Saul Bernstein, *Cityscapes*. Courtesy the artist.

Planes of the head isolated with line.

Light source from upper left.

Light source from lower right.

Light source from both upper left and upper right. All four illustrations by Saul Bernstein, courtesy the artist.

Thomas A. Leek, *Where Do We Come From? What Are We?*
Where Are We Going?, monochromatic wash drawing, 1986,
29" x 21" (73.5 x 53.5 cm)

Part 3

Portfolio

NEW DIRECTIONS in art do not progress in distinct sequences, neither do they begin and end abruptly. Each phase, rooted in the past, bears the seeds for change in the future. Regardless of newly acquired materials, concepts and styles, all movements inherit much from those that preceeded them.

This section presents a cross section of current work in the various fields of visual art. It is work that is not necessarily confined to galleries or to the exclusive domain of the fine arts. Examples of the personal, expressive work of art students, illustrators, commercial artists, cartoonists and other professional artists are represented.

Contemporary drawing is no longer restricted by conventional attitudes, a limited selection of materials and tools, or traditionally approved techniques. Diversity is the hallmark of today's "movements." The majority of current work, however, shows those qualities indispensable throughout the history of art and invulnerable to the seductive influence of contemporary cults.

Chapter 9

Contemporary

Drawing

One must not think that feeling is everything. Art is nothing without form.

Gustave Flaubert

ONE OF THE MOST provocative undertakings in both representational and nonobjective art is depicting a scattering of objects or random markings as they would appear either by accident or within uncontrolled circumstances. Thomas Leek (see p. 198) has symbolized a loosely grouped procession moving toward an indefinite destination. Impressions of distance, space and movement were attained through strategically planned visual devices. An elevated viewpoint was fixed by placing the horizon line near the top of the picture plane and adjusting the figures within a triangular perspective grid, based at the bottom of the design with its apex at a point near the horizon. Distance and space were indicated by progressively lightening the values and reducing the size of the figures as they approach the upper region of the picture plane. Motion was suggested by gently slanting the figures at various stages.

The artist often selects a medium for a particular physical quality that may be harmoniously combined with its support. A remarkable example is represented in Michael Wingo's drawing in which graphite and specially selected paper have been effectively united in producing an intriguing image. Both the concept and technique regarding the drawing are briefly noted by the artist:

I believe that art comes out of experience, both observed and felt. My drawing is part of an ongoing process based on personal intuition and a visual response that allows the drawing to guide me toward the "correct" visual solution. The composition and abstraction of the drawing continue to echo the theme of duality in this work—a visual paradox, if you will, much like human nature.

Michael Wingo's pen and ink drawing exhibits a provocative, whimsical quality. Its imagery, invented with hatch, limited crosshatch and linear markings, hovers between visual paradox and tangible reality. A clue to its origin and development is offered by the artist:

Pen (technical) and ink on a plate finish paper (12" x 14"). Imagery related to viewing invented landscape, symbolic of overcoming barriers via playful, witty forms. Technique: directly drawn, no preplanning. Hatching with line.

Michael Wingo, *Untitled,* **graphite, 8" x 24" (20.5 x 61 cm)**

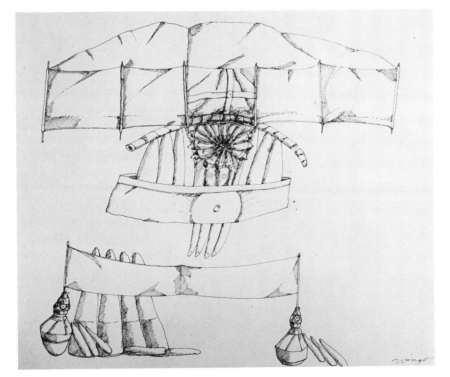

Michael Wingo, *Landscape,* **pen and ink, 12" x 14" (30.5 x 35.5 cm)**

Alan Zazlov, *Untitled*, mixed media, 18" x 23" (46 x 58.5 cm)

The recognizable images of a head and hands extended from outside the picture plane indicate that Alan Zazlov's drawing is fundamentally subjective. The viewer immediately is made aware of a draped figure with others, although unseen, in attendance nearby. The persuasive power of the design is derived from the *abstract,* twisting dynamics of drapery folds contained within a pattern based on the grid system near the center of the composition.

Subject and environment are conceived as a unit in Arnold Walter's black-and-white acrylic painting. The radial symmetry of the spider is extended to its web. Metaphorically, the bright faceted image of the spider, in contrast to the absolute blackness of the background, is reminiscent of a diamond in a velvety setting.

Cabbages presents a convoluted, organic quality. The rhythmic, linear and tonal patterns were developed indirectly. Jay Rivkin briefly comments on the concept and development of the piece:

Pencil drawing has always been the chamber music of the visual arts. As the lines and feelings are revealed, the process of drawing becomes fulfilling and unpredictable. Starting from a hard litho pencil and gradually working in toward the heavier and darker areas also produces that same feeling of surprise as the drawing develops. I have always been interested in taking the mundane and everyday objects we have around us and putting them into another area of heightened sensitivity. There is something intriguing in the idea, to me. I find, for example, the cabbage and its endless web of lines can keep me going for days on end, with hundreds of drawings, all looking quite different.

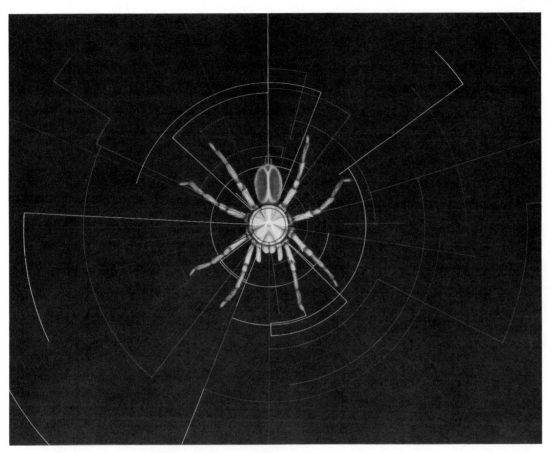

Arnold Walter, *Spider,* **acrylic, 36″ x 40″ (91.5 x 101.5 cm)**

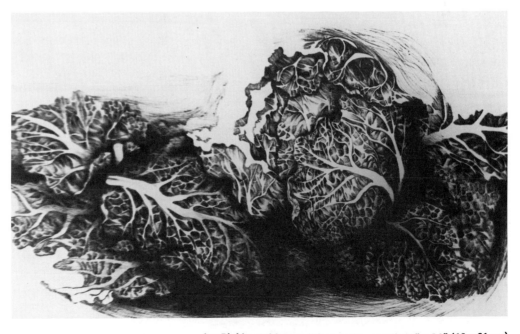

Jay Rivkin, *Cabbages,* **lithographic pencil, 18″ x 24″ (46 x 61 cm)**

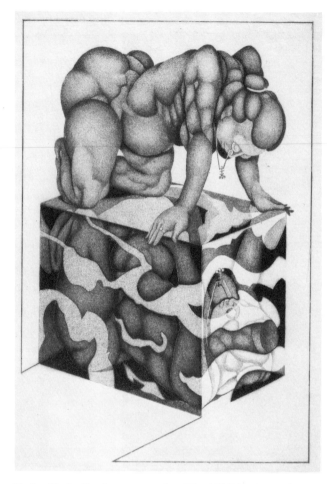

Marion Hyde, *Narcissus,* **engraving, 7" x 10" (18 x 25.5 cm)**

The etching by Venus Sobin reproduced in black and white demonstrates the importance of tonal values in color. The original image of the ape is printed with deep cadmium red, which registers at a low level of the tonal scale. The motif of the design was suggested by a verse, "The Ape and the Dolphin," from *Fables de la Fontaine.*

Venus Sobin, *Ape and Dolphin,* **etching, 24" x 28" (61 x 71 cm)**

A grotesque parody of the human figure has been masterfully drawn with an instrument only recently available. Marion Hyde developed the image on a zinc plate with an electric engraver, a device for marking or initialing metallic tools and equipment. Variations in line and tone are achieved by controlling pressures and the length of time the point is held and maneuvered in selected areas. Unlike the burin, which cuts an incisive line, the point of the electric engraver rapidly punches thousands of microdots into the surface of the metal plate to produce the image, which is later inked, run through a press and printed. The image in *Narcissus* was conceived as being contained within and extended upon two cubelike blocks shown in perspective. The invisible edges of the upper block closely contain a strongly contoured figure whose shattered, reflected image is extended on the sides of the lower block. The upper image is the result of contained form drawing with added perspective; the lower reflected image is based on the grid system for spatial composition.

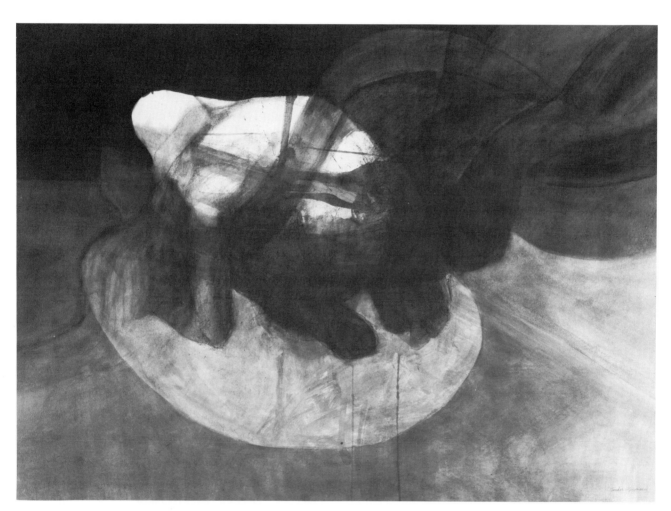

Tandra Jorgensen, *Night Victim,* mixed media, 29" x 40" (73.5 x 101.5 cm)

Expressing the essence of a sinister event requires graphic elements that stimulate a related response in the viewer. Regardless of the subject, a composition dominated by fused dark patterns tends to project somber, mysterious impressions. The *Disasters of War* series of etchings by Francisco Goya are classic examples in which the interplay of dark and light tonal passages, like those in *Night Victim* by Tandra Jorgensen, convey impressions of human tragedy.

A clue to the development of its design is offered by the artist:

The key to this composition is the interlocking shapes that create one dominating form. The interplay of contrasting values and the physical nature of the textures are important factors aimed at creating emotional tension.

Corinne West Hartley, *Young Girl,* **conte crayon, 18" x 24" (46 x 61 cm)**

The strongly lighted subject in Corinne West Hartley's crayon drawing exhibits a remarkable, tactful employment of diametrically opposed tonal values to depict and model the volumes and planes of the subject. The headdress, upper planes of the right arm and lower left arm, for example, have been shaped from the *outside* by vigorously applied black patterns. On the other hand, the left upper arm, the upper torso and the lateral plane of the lower left arm have been silhouetted against a stark white area.

Caroline Blake, *Title Holder,* conte wash, Crayola, 22" x 30" (56 x 76 cm)

Carmela Grunwaldt, *Untitled,* mixed media, 11½ x 9" (29 x 23 cm)

During the latter years of this century both abstract and minimal art have been recognized as valid expressive movements. Unfortunately their deceptively simplistic imagery has been adopted by many student-artists, either to conceal inept draftsmanship or as a convenient substitute for well-founded self-expression. Quality in abstract art requires a nearly infallible sense for aesthetic design, complete control of the medium being employed and a clear understanding of the expressive and aesthetic potentials of the visual elements. The aim of Carmela Grunwaldt's drawing is to plot areas on the picture plane to be transferred to a canvas, where the monochromatic shapes will be translated to the colors, textures and tonal values of an abstract painting.

Both dry and wet media have been employed by Caroline Blake in her drawing of a boxer. Placing the head of the subject near the top of the picture plane and forcing parts of the arm and lower half of the figure beyond its borders contribute a sense of monumentality to the composition. Following are statements by the artist:

Mixed media includes conte, charcoal and tortillion, diluted sepia wash on skin, diluted grey ink wash on shirt area over wax resist, sumi brush and ink line on gloves. I am concerned with shape placement (positive and negative) in overall composition as well as weight of line. Drawing is both interpretive and descriptive in this instance. A somewhat two-dimensional textural emphasis here grows out of an early love for Japanese drawings and prints. Apart from the object, style or content represented, good drawings have a life of their own, a recognizable vitality. A good drawing, however, may contain a minor flaw which makes it all the more real to me. Valid drawings, like other art forms, absorb, in varying measure, the artist's struggle to sustain or exceed the limits of craft and self. What occasionally transcends that struggle is the mystery that could be defined as art.

Beverly Worlock, *Telegraph Weeds,* **etching and aquatint, 13" x 21" (33 x 53.5 cm)**

Comments by the artist regarding the concept and development of the design follow:

This print is one of five commissioned to decorate the offices of a firm of landscape architects. Weeds were the somewhat tongue-in-cheek choice of subject matter. I made many realistic sketches from armloads of autumn-desiccated plant material and dozens of photographs made by my husband. The sketches evolved into stylized designs of black-and-white patterns against a dark background which I hoped would elevate these maligned shrubs and grasses into triumphant symbols of life rising Phoenixlike from the sun-baked California earth; life persisting in spite of man's encroachment. The designs were traced onto asphaltum-covered zinc plates, scratched with an etching needle to expose the metal, bitten with hydrochloric and nitric acids and printed in black ink using a hand-operated press.

These two motion picture illustrations by William Major are excellent examples of purposeful spatial organization restricted to specific dimensions. In this case the picture plane is proportioned to conform to a wide-angled film screen. The subjects of each, based on screenplays, are designed to provide key scenic images consistent with the theme of the story.

Space, monumentality, stability and motion are suggested in *Loves of Omar Khayyam* the white mountain slope occupying the upper left section of the composition serves as a backdrop for the dark figures entering the lower left portion of the picture plane. In contrast, the monumental visual impact of the dark escarpment was established by reducing the scale (size) and raising the tonal values of the column of riders moving along its base toward the right border of the scene.

A quiet, nostalgic event is suggested in *Desire under the Elms.* The gentle action of a trotting horse pulling a buggy is indicated within a subdued, peaceful setting. The effect was achieved by framing the dark, boldly stroked image of the moving subject within a transparent, broadly stroked environment.

The importance of location and proportion of a subject in relation to the picture plane is exhibited in Beverly Worlock's *Telegraph Weeds.* Within a vertically oriented rectangle, the subjects in the composition attain a status of dignity and stateliness. The impression is reinforced by lowering the horizon line toward the bottom of the picture plane.

William Major, *Loves of Omar Khayyam,* **wash drawing, 10" x 18" (25.5 x 46 cm)**

William Major, *Desire under the Elms,* **ink wash drawing, 10" x 18" (25.5 x 46 cm)**

A monotype is produced by placing a sheet of paper over a *wet* image developed on a metal, plastic or cardboard plate and running it through a press. When a press is not available, the artist may use a sheet of glass as the plate, in which case the image is transferred by rubbing the paper by hand after it has been placed over the image. Simonne Hulett adopted the monotype to suggest a dreamlike figure in a nocturnal landscape in *Navajo Woman in Moonlight.*

In spite of its title, *Penguins,* the fundamental theme of Kalman Schwartz's etching is based on the universally persuasive combination of black with white. In this case the total range of the light-and-dark value scale has been adopted.

Simonne Hulett, *Navajo Woman in Moonlight,* monotype, 18" x 24" (46 x 61 cm)

Kalman Schwartz, *Penguins,* etching, 16" x 12" (40.5 x 30.5 cm)

Thomas Leek, *Private Quarters*, india ínk and wash, 1986, 29¹/₈"
x 21¹/₈" (74 x 53.5 cm)

The content of Thomas Leek's drawing is more than a
graphic imitation of an observed subject. Symbolism is the
key to its design. Passing time is implied in the patina of
flaking paint. The creased, slightly askew window shade
without a curtain may be interpreted as an artifact of a
social condition, while the opaque darkness beyond the
shade symbolizes a mystery to be contemplated in the
mind of the viewer.

The high-keyed drawing by Lowell Northrop exemplifies a
composition in which the whiteness of the paper is assigned
a dominant role. The method requires that the quantity
(area) and the quality (intensity or purity) of whiteness
provided by the picture plane be carefully assessed and
judiciously spent. A dry medium, pencil, was sensitively
integrated with fibers of the paper to produce semitrans-
parent passages of tones and line through which the whiteness of the picture plane dominates the tonal elements of
the design.

**Lowell Northrop, *Figure Study*, pencil, 1985, 10" x 15" (25.5 x
38 cm)**

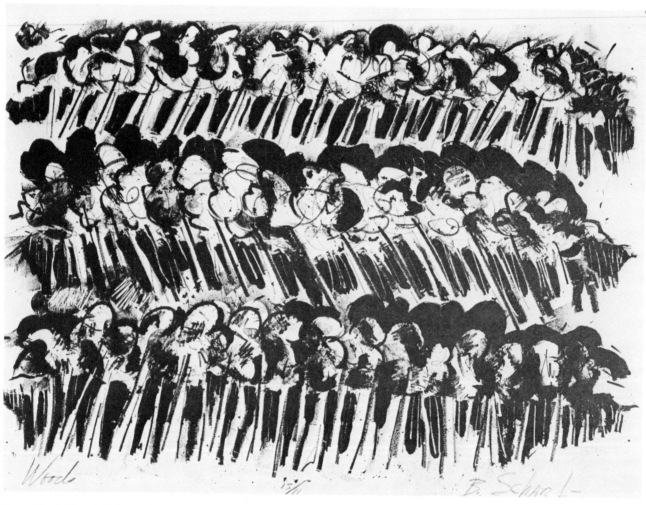

Barry Scharf, *Woods*, lithograph, 18" x 24" (46 x 61 cm)

Two drawings expressing different subjects, realized with different media, have something in common: *distinctive calligraphy*. Also, the untouched areas of the white surface are essential to the design in both drawings.

The staccato, vertically stroked pattern in Barry Scharf's lithograph was developed with tusche, comparable in viscosity and blackness to india ink. The drawing was developed by alternately lifting the brush from the surface and sensitively contacting it to complete each stroke. The approach is based on strokes similar to those adopted for calligraphic penmanship.

Terry Stout, *Delilah,* **oil crayon on newsprint, 18" x 24" (46 x 61 cm)**

Two versions of the element of line were adopted for Terry Stout's crayon drawing. One is the point-to-point approach where the points of the crayon were used to shape the contours of the head and its features. The other is the calligraphic approach where semicircular strokes based on radial symmetry represent the hair mass surrounding the head. Remarks by the artist regarding the drawing follow:

The intent of this work is to stress the uniqueness of a single human being. To accomplish this I used contour line segments in conjunction with multiple viewpoint so that each feature is unique; that is, the left eye is distinctly different from the right eye and not just a schematic or a reversal. The same applies to the exaggeration of fact. The human face only appears symmetrical. It is not. As individual human features are unique, so are individual human beings. In similarity there is diversity.

Rosita Tsue, *The Intruder,* **sumi wash on rice paper, 12" x 23" (30.5 x 58.5 cm)**

In Rosita Tsue's drawing the brush was seldom lifted from the paper. Variations in line and tone were achieved by changing the pressures and speeds of the brush while it was being manipulated.

Winnie Hawkins, *Reflections of Learning*, watercolor and gouache, 20" x 32" (51 x 81 cm)

The options offered by any medium, including watercolor, either by itself or combined with others, may be explored and utilized. Winnie Hawkins has combined the opaque quality of gouache with accents of transparent watercolor in *Reflections of Learning*. Large transparent washes are absent in its design; however, the unique chromatic intensity of watercolor has been employed within the interlocking sections of the horizontal pattern extending across the middle of the picture plane. According to the artist:

Titles and ideas for paintings are always in mind. The titles remain constant, but the images of the painting change. I work from an abstract drawing, often using some sort of a grid for stability. Subjects are found mostly in reality, but many times come from my imagination. I begin a painting with an abstract underpainting of watercolor. With glazes I develop the subject matter, such as it is. Then I am not happy until line is woven throughout. This is my world as I see it. However I do not want to make it so completely personal that the viewer cannot also find his or her world in it and understand and enjoy it within his or her own frame of reference.

The expressive and aesthetic potentials of watercolor, like ink wash, depend to a great degree on the quality of transparency. B. J. White has used wide, freely applied strokes of transparent watercolor to trap or isolate an undulating paper-white shape extending horizontally across the upper region of the picture plane. The optically attractive interplay between the *opaque* white band and the *transparent* washes contributes an important textural element to the design. A brief summary by the artist:

The series of small paintings entitled Landscape Patterns *evolved from sketches jotted down while traveling. The sketches were later combined, rearranged and painted in the studio. The painting began by layering or glazing color, structuring the shapes. Many techniques were explored in order to achieve a simple texture for the complexity of the foreground. In this instance, paper was laid in wet pigment and allowed to dry. In my paintings I feel that by eliminating detail and consolidating the interplay of patterns to simple shapes, the relationships have more impact.*

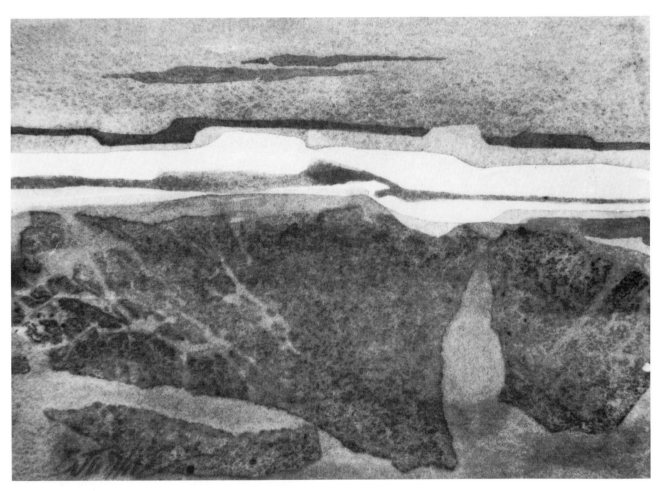

B. J. White, *Landscape Patterns,* **transparent watercolor, 5¹/₂″ x
7¹/₂″ (14 x 19 cm)**

Sylvia Stolzberg, *Study,* **oil wash, 9" x 12" (23 x 30.5 cm)**

Manuel De Leon, *Untitled,* **burnt umber chalk and conte crayon, 30" x 40" (76 x 101.5 cm)**

The points, edges and sides of the elongated cubelike crayon have been employed in the drawing by Manuel De Leon. It was completed before an audience to demonstrate the versatility of a dry medium. The higher values of the light-and-dark value scale were used to represent the lighted planes of the figure and its garments. The lower values indicate the color of the hair, the skirt and the darker planes of the figure, including details of the head.

One of the objectives of Sylvia Stolzberg's *Study* was to exploit the effect of capillary attraction when brushstrokes, heavily charged with thinned oil pigments, are integrated with highly absorbent fibers of watercolor paper. In this drawing the element of line is practically absent. Tone and texture are the featured elements.

A sketch may serve as a study for a major work of art or it may be completed for its own sake. Regardless of its origin or purpose, a sketch is a quickly executed, intuitively directed drawing that often displays qualities lacking in works fastidiously produced over longer periods of time. The charcoal sketch by Martin Mondrus was realized with minimal stroking within the limited area of a notebook page during a brief period of time.

A dated photograph album inspired Wilda Northrop's nostalgic sketch. Brisk strokes of a soft pencil, indicating the background located within the left and upper areas of the picture plane, were also used to surround and shape the figures in the left foreground and suggest the local color of the garments worn by the figures at the right.

Wilda Northrop, *Paul's on the Running Board,* **pencil, 1983, 14"
x 18" (35.5 x 46 cm)**

Martin Mondrus, *Fallen Giant,* **charcoal, 10" x 18" (25.5 x 46 cm)**

Ethel Fisher, *476 Broome St.—N.Y.C., 1976*, graphite, 14" x 20" (35.5 x 51 cm)

The pencil drawing by Ethel Fisher displays a sense for aesthetic spatial organization, effective integration of a dry medium with textured surface, and skillful maintenance of values within a narrow range of the tonal scale. A brief comment by the artist regarding the practical as well as conceptual factors involved follows:

The drawing is on 14" x 20" rough Arches watercolor paper, 140 pound weight. The graphite pencils used, from very light 9H to rich, dark 2B. The original is traced onto the Arches paper, then I work thousands of small pencil strokes into the fibers of the rough paper. It gives the effect of a bonding to the support. The main concern was with space and values, an extension of my own painting concerns. I used my own photographs and the reality around me.

Ida Bernstein's art thoughtfully pursues hidden drama in common human events. The tonal values of the etching, which extend from the lowest to the highest of the dark-and-light scale, project a sense of stillness, quietness and peace.

Ida Bernstein, *Walking*, etching and aquatint, 5" x 5" (12.5 x 12.5 cm)

Ron Adams, *Self-Portrait,* **lithograph, 52" x 30" (132 x 76 cm)**

With the exception of the position of the design on the picture plane, which is reversed to its mirror image during printing, the graphic quality of a lithographic design remains exactly as it is drawn on the surface of a stone or metallic plate. The emphasis on realism in Ron Adam's *Self-Portrait* inspired the artist to include the implements used for its development. However, the requirements for expressive and aesthetic composition prompted the artist to rearrange the objects to serve as active counterpoints to the stable image of the figure. The tonal composition is based on a nearly equally balanced version of chiaroscuro with the darks assuming the principal role.

Gerald Richman, *Margie,* **conte and charcoal, 38" x 48" (96.5 x 122 cm)**

Both of the drawings by Gerald Richman demonstrate remarkable control of the elongated cubelike charcoal stick and conte crayon. In *Margie* the head, projected arms and rounded sleeve have been stated with the broad sides of both charcoal and conte crayon, while their long bladelike edges were used to represent the upper half of the figure, add detail to the head and establish the vertical thrusts of the gravity folds in the garment. The artist comments:

This is simply a charcoal and conte crayon study of a friend.

The broad sides of compressed charcoal were used in *Dead Seagull* to indicate the tonal values of wings and feathers. The thin, elongated edges were rotated to suggest the volumes, planes and general structure of the subject. The artist comments:

On my way past the Monastery Beach I saw this dead seagull. The bird was a lump lying in the sand. Occasionally the wind would move the upper wing which gave me a feeling of the past and the soaring it would do no more. A young boy came by and asked, "Why are you drawing a dead bird?" Without thought I replied, "Because it interests me." Later I realized that was the best answer I could have given.

Gerald Richman, *Dead Seagull,* **conte and charcoal, 16" x 20" (40.5 x 51 cm)**

Epilogue

To see a World in a grain of Sand
And a Heaven in a Wild Flower,
Hold Infinity in the palm of your hand
And Eternity in an hour.
William Blake

THE MAIN OBJECTIVE of this book has been to present and demonstrate procedures to help you understand the inherent conceptual factors and master the practical methods that determine the expressive and aesthetic potentials of visual art. These fundamental skills can be realized through the analytical and expressive process we know as drawing. Art that has stimulated the major movements in art history and survived periods of decline is founded on proven basic principles and factors that, to a great degree, have been conceived and realized through draftsmanship. Some key factors that have served as guidelines for the conservative artist as well as the speculative innovator are reviewed here:

1. The importance of drawing may best be understood, appreciated and utilized if it is perceived as an inherent method of communication that is universally comprehended and through which the expressive and aesthetic qualities of art may be achieved.

2. The scope of draftsmanship and its potentials encompasses more than the skill to render an authentic-appearing two-dimensional version of three-dimensional reality. The difference that separates creative, expressive draftsmanship from technical proficiency is the ability to reinterpret purposefully with the mind, images perceived by the eye and brain and to suggest imagery beyond the domain surveyed by the sense of sight.

3. The adoption of the idealized human figure as an aesthetic standard is not the result of an arbitrary decision by either an influential individual or group, it is a natural historical legacy. It seems difficult to conceive of an alternative structure that more ideally embodies the basic principles of art: *functional design and harmonious integration of its components.*

4. The elements of visual art remain constant regardless of the medium through which they are employed. For example, line and tone produce similar effects whether they are drawn with pencil or pen on paper, brushed on canvas or etched in metal. The distinguishing factor is limited to the sensual effect stimulated in the viewer by the physical nature of the medium and the surface on which it is applied.

5. Durable, lasting movements in the field of art occur infrequently and are not easily established. Many new directions hailed by critics and scholars are eventually judged either as spurious attempts to attract attention or as expedient ways to avoid the concerns and disciplines involved in the production of significant work. The true dissident breaks with tradition not to avoid its demands, but because he or she is left with no alternative. Usually the innovator harbors inner disciplines more rigid and nonconforming than those that are rejected.

Whether or not art can be taught or is conceived through an inherent propensity traditionally referred to as talent, has been and will continue to be an insoluble issue. Satisfactory definitions of art and talent are not only unattainable, they are neither desirable nor necessary. Art is not a science, yet the principles and theories through which it may be realized, and the proven methods for controlling its media, can be successfully taught.

Through training, study and accumulated knowledge we have discovered routes to an undefined boundary within the human mind that separates physical reality from the intangible mystery of art. It is within the uncultivated, uncharted wilderness of the human mind that the muses of art exist and the creative process takes place. The theories and practical experiments in this book offer a guide to that frontier.

Index

Acknowledgments

I deeply appreciate the encouragement, advice and practical assistance that various individuals and institutions have generously contributed toward the production of this book. I am indebted to:

My wife, who as a patient, discerning critic helped in establishing a practical arrangement of the book and in maintaining consistency of theme.

Skip Takeuchi, who photographed most of the illustrated material contained in the book.

Beverly Worlock, artist and teacher, who, being familiar with the theories and techniques presented in the book, contributed many valid suggestions essential for integrating the text, concepts and techniques.

Joseph Gatto, colleague and friend, who periodically advised me on the conceptual and editorial aspects of book production.

Marie Starr for categorizing the material during the development of the book.

Gerald Brommer and Albert Porter for their critical assessment of the outline and theme during the formative stage.

Sam Rudnick, Ernest Gardetto, Robert Worlock and the many friends whose comments regarding the theme and text aided me immeasurably.

Saul Bernstein for demonstrating the aesthetic and expressive potentials of computer art.

Michael Darr for explaining the technical aspects of the computer.

Lori Wolfson who helped organize material in the intial chapters.

The following resources for access to their extensive collections of visual art:

Limited Editions and Heritage Press, New York, New York
Dallas Museum of Art, Dallas, Texas
National Gallery of Art, Washington, D.C.
Norton Simon Museum of Art, Pasadena, California
Museum of Modern Art, New York, New York
Los Angeles County Museum of Art, Los Angeles, California
Museum of Fine Art, Boston, Massachusetts
Los Angeles *Examiner,* Los Angeles, California
Joseph Gatto Collection, Los Angeles, California
Golden State Mutual Collection, Los Angeles, California
Art Center School of Design, Pasadena, California